Amigurumi!

Super Happy Crochet Cute

Amigurumi!

Super Happy Crochet Cute

Elisabeth A. Doherty

LARK BOOKS

A Division of Sterling Publishing Co., Inc.

New York / London

Senior Editor
Valerie Van Arsdale Shrader

Technical Editor
Donna Druchunas

Technical Consultant
K.J. Hay

Art Director
Stacey Budge

Cover Designer
Cindy LaBreacht

Associate Editor
Nathalie Mornu

Associate Designer
Travis Medford

Art Production Assistant
Jeff Hamilton

Editorial Assistance
Cassie Moore

Editorial Intern
Katrina Usher

Art Intern
Michael Foreman

Illustrators
Orrin Lundgren
Travis Medford

Photographer
Stewart O'Shields

Dedication
To Jane and Terry—this book would have never happened without them…Hmm, I give myself ideas.

Library of Congress Cataloging-in-Publication Data

Doherty, Elisabeth A., 1980-
  Amigurumi! : super happy crochet cute / Elisabeth A. Doherty. -- 1st ed.
    p. cm.
  Includes index.
  ISBN-13: 978-1-60059-017-7 (pb-trade pbk. : alk. paper)
  ISBN-10: 1-60059-017-9 (pb-trade pbk. : alk. paper)
  1. Dollmaking. 2. Crocheting. I. Title.
  TT175.D568 2007
  746.43'4041--dc22
                                                    2007007175

10 9 8 7 6 5 4 3 2 1

First Edition

Published by Lark Books, A Division of
Sterling Publishing Co., Inc.
387 Park Avenue South, New York, N.Y. 10016

Text © 2007, Elisabeth A. Doherty
Photography © 2007, Lark Books unless otherwise specified
Illustrations © 2007, Lark Books unless otherwise specified
Illustration (Screaming Girl logo) on pages 7, 37, 39, 43, 49, 56, 64, 72, 85, 89, 99, 108, and 117
© 2007, Elisabeth A. Doherty

Distributed in Canada by Sterling Publishing,
c/o Canadian Manda Group, 165 Dufferin Street
Toronto, Ontario, Canada M6K 3H6

Distributed in the United Kingdom by GMC Distribution Services,
Castle Place, 166 High Street, Lewes, East Sussex, England BN7 1XU

Distributed in Australia by Capricorn Link (Australia) Pty Ltd.,
P.O. Box 704, Windsor, NSW 2756 Australia

If you have questions or comments about this book, please contact:
Lark Books
67 Broadway
Asheville, NC 28801
(828) 253-0467

Manufactured in China

ISBN 13: 978-1-60059-017-7
ISBN 10: 1-60059-017-9

For information about custom editions, special sales, premium and corporate purchases, please contact Sterling Special Sales Department at 800-805-5489 or specialsales@sterlingpub.com.

Table of Contents

Introduction 6

Materials 8

Stitches and Techniques 16

Gauge 32

Tasty Tidbits 34

Not-So-Crunchy Carrot 35
Fresh Strawberries 38
Sandwich Cookie 41
Cutecakes 44
Cheeseburger with the Works 47
Skelly Fish 55

Further Along the Food Chain 60

Mighty L'il Mouse 61
Werner the Wiener Dog 65
Piglet 73
Friends Forever Fawn 79

Humanoids 86

Hep Cat 87
Benny the Monkey 97
Punk Bunny 106
Strawbeary 115

Taking Care of Your Hands 126

Templates 127

Author Bio 128

Index 128

Introduction

What in the world could possess a sane person to crochet a doll? I told someone about my artwork recently and she said, with a look of disgust on her face, "You mean those dolls that you put on top of toilet paper?!?"

"No," I told her, "not *those* dolls."

I'm as surprised as anyone that my creative pursuits have led me to doll making, which is, let's face it, a borderline activity even when they're not being used to hide unsightly bathroom items. Even the sweetest baby doll makes me think of poppets, effigies, and voodoo dolls with their little bits of real human hair, skin, and nails. They just creep me out.

Then we have the whole sordid history of crochet itself to deal with. Crochet means hook in French. This makes sense because, obviously, crochet is done with a hook. But some argue that the term has a double meaning, given to the craft because prostitutes—hookers—practiced it. It's likely that it was given a bad name by the aristocracy because it was a cheap way to reproduce lace that previously was only attainable by the very rich.

So there we have it, a double whammy against the craft you and I are interested in doing. One, doll making is sort of spooky and two, crochet is the disgusting stepchild of the craft world. Well, maybe that title really belongs to macramé, but we won't go there.

So why has this craft that should be repugnant suddenly become so appealing? Enter Japanese pop culture, which has the power to make just about anything cool. In Japan a crocheted or knitted doll is called an *amigurumi* (ah-mee-guh-ROO-mee). Disclaimer: Please people, I do not speak Japanese. This pronunciation guide should be taken with a grain of salt. There is very little information available in English on amigurumi, so I have decided to go with my own definition based on information I found in an online encyclopedia. *Ami* is a shortening of the word *amimie*, which means "stitch." *Gurumi* is a shortening of the word *nuigurumi*, which means "stuffed doll or toy." Smoosh the two together and you get amigurumi.

No doubt you'll have noticed these dolls look different from those garish bathroom haunts. For the most part amigurumi are *kawaii*, which is Japanese for cute. The nose-wrinkling sort-of "Oh, my gosh, that is so cute!" cute. The kind of cute that master's students write dark, heavy theses about. But you don't have to worry about the deep social implications this kind of cute has in order to enjoy making these dolls. Thank goodness.

So how did an Irish-American Chicagoan start making these dolls with the Japanese name? Around February '05 I got a bizarre migraine headache that triggered an episode of amnesia. I already knew how to crochet before getting sick and had made a doll or two after seeing some on Craftster.org—this whole phenomenon has a huge life online. When I got back from the hospital, tired and needing a break, I thought amigurumi would be a good way to express myself without all of the heavy emotional baggage that the paintings I had previously been concentrating on carried with them. Since then I have had so many ideas for new creatures that I just haven't had the chance to get back to painting.

So the patterns in this book are my original designs, developed since the amnesia. This should be encouraging to those of you who may feel nervous about your crafting abilities; if my addled brain can come up with them, you can certainly make them. In the sections that follow you'll become acquainted with the broad range of fabulous materials you'll be using to make the amigurumi, as well as the techniques you'll need to get started. The patterns are presented in three separate chapters. They are broken down by approximate level of difficulty. If you're a complete beginner, try starting out with the Tasty Tidbits and moving through the patterns in order, building your skills as you go so that you'll be ready for the more challenging patterns at the end of the book.

Whether you're a novice or an expert stitcher, please enjoy yourself. Love your creation because you made it.

Backstory

Look for little blog-style posts throughout the book for random thoughts, tips, and stories behind the projects.

7

Materials

Mmm...materials. Let's face it, they're the reason many of us do the crafts we do. Just the other day my mom, who has been doing artwork in pencil for the past few years, came over to my studio and I showed her the new sequins I ordered from an online specialty shop. She oohed and aahed for a few minutes looking at the iridescent flowers and butterflies and finally said, "I think I'm working in the wrong medium." But before you rush off to buy trimmings for amigurumis that don't exist yet, let's talk about the basic supplies you need to make your yarn babies come to life.

Hooks

Hooks are what make this needlecraft unique, for goodness sake, so we might as well get this portion of our supply list correct. For these amigurumi you'll be working at a very tight gauge. This is a scenario just begging for tired, crampy hands. I urge you to invest the extra few dollars in what are called ergonomic hooks. They have a padded, plastic grip that's much more comfortable than a skinny metal shaft. They're rigid, unlike the completely plastic hooks that will bend all over the place if you try to force them into the very tight fabric you're about to make. They have lovely, smooth anodized aluminum tips that are pointier than most others I have encountered and go in and out of your handiwork without a hitch. Most hobby stores carry these. I discovered these wonderful hooks shortly after beginning my crochet odyssey and am a complete convert. If a regular hook is like a battery-operated, remote-controlled car, an ergonomic hook is like an Italian racing machine.

Crochet Hook Letter Sizes & Metric Equivalents

There are several different numbering systems for crochet hook sizes, depending upon the material and the manufacturer. The metric system is the only constant measurement scale and is now often included along with the size indicator on each hook.

Yarn Hooks

U.S. Size	Metric
B-1	2.25 mm
C-2	2.75 mm
D-3	3.25 mm
E-4	3.50 mm
F-5	3.75 mm
G-6	4.00 mm
7	4.50 mm
H-8	5.00 mm
I-9	5.50 mm
J-10	6.00 mm
K-10 1/2	6.50 mm
L-11	8.00 mm
M/N-13	9.00 mm
N/P-15	10.00 mm

Steel Hooks

U.S. Size	Metric
00	3.50 mm
0	3.25 mm
1	2.75 mm
2	2.25 mm
3	2.10 mm
4	2.00 mm
5	1.90 mm
6	1.80 mm
7	1.65 mm
8	1.50 mm
9	1.40 mm
10	1.30 mm
11	1.10 mm
12	1.00 mm
13	0.85 mm
14	0.75 mm

Yarn

And now for the yarn. You would look pretty goofy doing crochet stitches in the air without yarn attached, wouldn't you? Many committed garment makers will be utterly scandalized by what I am about to say, so this is your warning. Worsted weight acrylic yarn is the absolute best yarn, hands down, for making amigurumi.

Now, wait a second, give me a chance to explain myself. It is indeed the very reason that you hate this yarn so much for making sweaters that makes it perfect for amigurumi: it has no stretch. Once you knit or crochet it into a shape there is almost no way of getting it out of that shape. The patterns for the little dolls you are about to make contain detailed shaping instructions, and you can completely destroy the shape by overstuffing if you use stretchy wool yarn. Believe me, I have seen it happen. But the stubborn acrylic yarn holds its shape beautifully.

Now let me explain which acrylic yarn I am talking about. Since the sixties and seventies when you or your mother were making all of those lovely afghans out of "super saver" this and "one pounder" that, there have been some marvelous advances in the world of plastics.

Estimating Yarn Amounts

Most of the parts of the amigurumis require only small amounts of yarn. If you have a stash and leftover scrap yarn, you probably won't have to purchase much yarn for these projects. Here are a few tips to help you figure out how much you'll need of each color.

For the small food items and the embellishments on the animals and humanoids, you'll be able to use scrap yarn left over from other projects. The smallest patches of a single color won't take more than 5 or 10 yards (4.6 to 9.1 m) of yarn. And these items are so quick to crochet that even if you run out of yarn, it's not a big deal to start over. The larger pieces, like the lettuce on the cheeseburger and the pants on the humanoids, won't take more than 25 yards (22.9 m) or so. When you need a color that you don't have in your stash, one ball will be enough to make many small pieces.

For the main color of the animals and humanoids, having one skein of yarn is not a bad idea. In most cases, you'll be able to make a couple of 'gurumis with that skein of yarn.

There are lines of acrylic yarn for sale now that have the words "soft" or "satin" in their names. This is no marketing gimmick. They are fluffy as a cloud and shiny, exactly what you want for your amigurumis. They give wonderful stitch definition so you'll be able to tell straight off if you have made a mistake. Best of all, they come in an absolute rainbow of colors. Colors that you would never let yourself spend a small fortune on to make a sweater out of, but heck, one skein of these yarns costs less than a fancy coffee drink. You can buy every color the company makes if you want to and not feel (too) guilty.

Stuffing

Stuffing—you can't have a stuffed animal without it. This seems straightforward enough, but the world of stuffing can be confusing. It goes by many names: stuffing, fiberfill, polyfill, polystuffing. These are all pretty much the same thing as far as I have been able to determine. Just don't buy wool or cotton, and don't buy batting. That is the flat stuff for putting in quilts.

The good news is that it's not necessary to buy the best of the best. You may be tempted by the expensive cluster-type stuffing, but don't spend your money there. The crocheted fabric is going to be so thick that you won't be able to appreciate your investment. This product is better reserved for delicate, sewn toys. You just want to buy stuffing that is easy enough to work with so it won't bunch up on you instantly. I am not particularly brand loyal here. I just go to the craft store and buy the second cheapest filling. I stuff my 'gurumis firmly, so one 12oz (340 g) bag usually only fills two or three dolls.

Even if you take your time and do Zen meditational breathing while stuffing your 'gurumi with the most expensive brand of poyfill you can find, it will still bunch. That is just the nature of stuffing. You can only handle it so much before it dies. A dead piece looks more like the end of a cotton swab than the piece of fluff you pulled out of the bag. You will be able to feel it distinctly from the outside of the crocheted fabric, sort of like the princess and the pea. If you suspect the bit of stuffing you are working with is dead just throw it away and start with a new piece, as there's no hope for it. Learning when to throw away dead polyfill just takes practice.

At some point, you'll probably be exasperated by stuffing the small arm or tail of a 'gurumi and be tempted to buy a stuffing tool. Don't bother. They're a waste of money for 'gurumi making. Try the end of a stick pen or knitting needle instead. Most of all, for these small pieces, I recommend you stuff them as you crochet them. For example, when an arm is halfway completed take a break to stuff down into the hand and up into the wrist a bit so you won't have to struggle with getting stuffing all the way down there later.

Another fun filling to use is the PVC pellet. This inorganic alternative to dried beans can be found at most craft stores. Please don't ever use dried beans. Just think: your doll gets wet, the acrylic yarn recovers, the polyfill recovers, but the beans sprout and all of your hard work is ruined. Your lovely doll looks like it has some sort of terrible gut-eating worm bursting from its belly. Just don't do it, folks!

To put a bit of weight in a doll's belly, I like to make a little sack out of half of a knee-high nylon that I buy at the drug store and fill it with a small handful of the pellets. Then I put it in the doll along with the polyfill. The pellets are also useful for weighting the legs of dolls that might not otherwise stand up.

Here's a serious note: Don't put PVC pellets in dolls you are giving to small children, because the pellets are very small and may represent a choking hazard.

Notions

As with all needlework projects, you'll find a variety of notions useful.

Locking stitch markers are a lifesaver. I use the type that look like a plastic safety pin. Although it might seem like a bit of a pain to lock and unlock the marker every time you need to move it, believe me, this is nothing compared to the pain of having a split ring marker suddenly abandon ship, leaving you with no earthly clue as to where you were.

In addition to keeping track of where you are with a marker, you'll also need some means of counting. How you do this is completely up to you. Some people like counters, some don't. Some people write in their books, some don't.

I recommend having a small pair of **pointed scissors** on hand. These certainly don't have to be expensive, just small and sharp enough so that when you're trimming ends you can get very close to your work without damaging it.

You'll also need a variety of **needles**. One of them, of course, for yarn, but also one for regular sewing. If you're going to embellish your doll, you'll need a beading needle and an embroidery needle as well.

Large, blunt pins, like knitting seaming pins, are very handy to keep around. I use these to keep ears and arms in place while deciding where they will ultimately go. The heads are big enough so they won't get lost in the crochet and the shafts are wide enough so they'll hold the item you are pinning quite securely.

Embellishments

Now we're getting down to the fun stuff, the supplies that will bring your amigurumi to life.

Eyes

Most appropriate to address first seems the eyes, windows of the soul, you know. Unfortunately, doll eyes can be painfully difficult to find. If you get lucky, they'll be in stock at your local hobby store. I never rely on providence, so I usually order eyes online. The eyes used in this book are acrylic, with shafts on the back that you poke through the crochet. Some of the shafts are very wide so you'll need something pointier to go into the head first. I use a rattail comb— really! Then a washer attaches on the back. The eyes come both in solid black and with irises. If you're making a doll for a young child, look for child-safety eyes.

13

Perle Cotton

Perle cotton has become such an essential part of my dolls that I decided to give it its own paragraph. Perle cotton is wonderful and versatile. Its shine matches that of the yarn you'll be using and it comes in a wide variety of colors. You can use it to embroider the faces on the 'gurumis, and the details on their clothes, and the felt patches that some of the doll patterns include. You can actually crochet with Perle cotton to create the small pieces that embellish some of the dolls. Don't be intimidated by the small steel hook you will have to use. Your grandmother used much smaller ones to make lace with. And who knows—you might love it! Before you know it your house may be covered in doilies. Perle cotton can usually be found on the embroidery aisle of the hobby store. It's near the embroidery floss, but don't confuse it with embroidery floss, which is duller and harder to work with. Perle cotton is spun tightly so it won't come apart when you crochet with it. Regular embroidery floss is meant to come apart, and if you try to crochet with it you may become frustrated at its tendency to split and fray.

Sparkle

And now we come to the **sequins** portion of our show. These trimmings, and other bits, make up the proverbial icing on the 'gurumi cake. Sometimes all a doll needs is the perfect bit of sparkle here or small detail there to finish it off and make it wonderful. Each pattern will tell you what you need to finish off your 'gurumi as I did, but for now here's a taste of what is to come, along with some other ideas not contained in specific patterns. These additional ideas are here to help you add your own flair to your creations, and to help you start thinking along the lines that anything can be used for these dolls as long as it can be attached to them in some way, although I don't recommend using an excess of glue.

Rayon embroidery floss is perfect for thick, shiny eyelashes.

Delica beads are great for making the ends of those eyelashes look wider and sparkly. I love to use **size 8 seed beads** for monkey nostrils. They are exactly the right size. Really. I use them any place I would put a French knot if I were good enough at doing French knots that I was confident they wouldn't pull out over time.

Sparkly blending filament, found near the cross-stitching supplies at the craft store, can be added to any yarn to make it fun and shiny without changing the weight.

Novelty yarn can be used for making wigs, grass skirts, monster fur, etc.

Ribbon can serve as a belt or a tie.

The scrapbooking aisle has **cute little brads** that I use for snaps on Mary Janes. There are **mini buttons** on this aisle, too.

Wool felt is great for making little pockets and patches. (Acrylic craft felt doesn't have the same body and texture, and just doesn't look as good.) Some of you who don't like working with tiny crochet hooks might want to try cutting eye patches out of this.

Fabric scraps can be skirts and bandanas.

Attaching embellishments is easy.
Clear nylon thread (also called invisible thread) for machine sewing is my favorite thing for attaching most embellishments that need to be sewn on. It is a bit tough to use at first but definitely worth it because you don't have to hide your stitches. **Craft glue** is great for attaching felt, but as I said before, glue should be used sparingly.

You should feel free to try anything that can be attached to your amigurumi as an embellishment. The most important thing to keep in mind is scale. The largest doll you will be making is only about 15 inches (38.1cm) tall, so keep the embellishments on the small side and it will all be good.

Stitches and Techniques

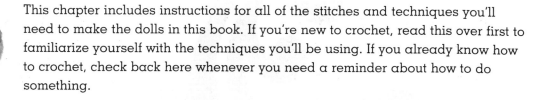

This chapter includes instructions for all of the stitches and techniques you'll need to make the dolls in this book. If you're new to crochet, read this over first to familiarize yourself with the techniques you'll be using. If you already know how to crochet, check back here whenever you need a reminder about how to do something.

Getting Started

The foundation of all crochet projects is either a length of chain (ch) stitches or a ring. You'll crochet the rows or rounds (rnds) of your project on top of this foundation.

Chain Stitch

A foundation chain is used to start many pieces of crochet. Chains are also worked when turning at the beginning of some rows and rounds.

1. Make a slipknot on your hook.

2. Holding your hook, bring the yarn over the hook from back to front.

3. Bring the yarn through the loop (lp) on your hook.

You've made one chain stitch. Repeat steps 2 and 3 over and over again. As you make new chain stitches, move your thumb and middle finger—of the hand not holding the hook—up to hold the work (figure 1).

Tip: Be sure to work your stitches on the thickest part of the crochet hook between where you grasp the hook and the end of the hook. This will ensure that your stitches aren't too tight.

Figure 1

Counting Chain Stitches

As you crochet a chain, it's essential to count the number of stitches you've made. You'll notice that your chain has two distinct sides. The front of the chain—the right side (RS)—should appear as a series of well-defined V-shapes. The wrong side (WS) appears as a series of small bumpy loops. Hold the chain with the right side of the chain stitches facing you. Start counting with the last stitch you completed (not the one on your hook) and don't count the slipknot you made at the beginning of the chain (figure 2).

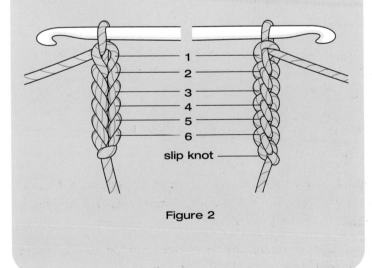

Figure 2

Make Ring

To crochet in the round, you'll need to make a ring (mr) as a foundation for your stitches. (See page 24 for more information on crocheting in rounds.)

1. Make a loop by putting the yarn tail behind the yarn coming from the skein, leaving a 4-inch (10 cm) tail (figure 3).

2. Use the hook to pull the working yarn through the loop (figure 4)—one loop is now on the hook (figure 5).

After you've made your ring, begin to work the first round as instructed in the pattern. In most cases, you will chain one, then make a number of single crochet stitches into the ring.

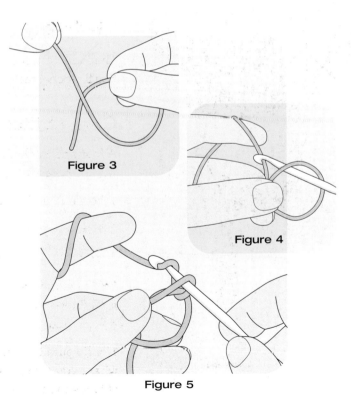

Figure 3

Figure 4

Figure 5

Crochet Stitches

Now let's talk about the stitches themselves.

Slip Stitch

Slip stitch (sl st) is a simple stitch that adds little or no height to a crocheted piece. It is often used to join rounds (see page 24) when crocheting circular pieces.

1. Insert the hook into the next stitch.

2. Bring the yarn over (YO) the hook, catch the working yarn, and pull the hook through the stitch and the loop on your hook (figure 6). This completes one slip stitch. One loop remains on the hook.

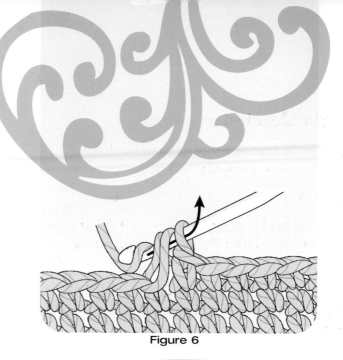

Figure 6

18

Single Crochet

Single crochet (sc) is the short basic stitch that's used most often in the projects in this book.

1. Insert the hook into the next stitch (figure 7).

2. Bring the yarn over the hook and pull the working yarn through the stitch (figure 8). You now have two loops on your hook.

3. Bring the yarn over the hook again and pull the yarn through both loops (figure 9). This completes one single crochet. One loop remains on the hook.

Reverse Single Crochet (Crab Stitch)

Just as the name implies, you work this stitch just as you do a regular single crochet—except in reverse. You work this stitch from left to right. This stitch is used most frequently for creating a decorative edge on your completed work.

1. Insert the hook into the next stitch to the right of your hook (figure 10).

2. Bring the yarn over the hook and pull the yarn through the stitch (figure 11).

3. Yarn over and pull the yarn through both loops (figure 12). You've completed one reverse single crochet. One loop remains on the hook.

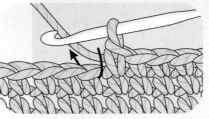

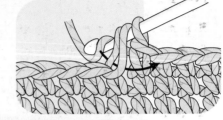

Figure 7

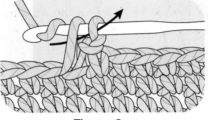

Figure 8

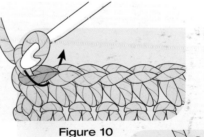

Figure 9

Figure 10

Figure 11

19

Double Crochet

Double crochet (dc) is about twice as tall as single crochet.

1. Bring the yarn over the hook and insert the hook into the next stitch (figure 13).

2. Bring the yarn over the hook and pull the yarn through the stitch. Three loops are on the hook (figure 14).

3. Yarn over and pull the yarn through the first two loops on the hook (figure 15). Two loops remain on the hook.

4. Yarn over and pull the yarn through the last two loops on the hook (figure 16). You've completed one double crochet stitch. One loop remains on the hook.

Half Double Crochet

Half double crochet (hdc) is slightly shorter than a double crochet and taller than a single crochet.

1. Bring the yarn over the hook and insert the hook into the next stitch (figure 17).

2. Yarn over and pull the yarn through the stitch. You should have three loops on the hook (figure 18).

3. Yarn over and pull the yarn through the three loops on the hook (figure 19). You've completed one half double crochet stitch. One loop remains on the hook.

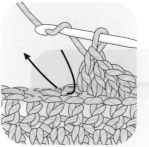

Figure 13

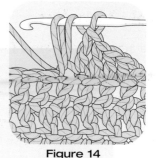

Figure 14

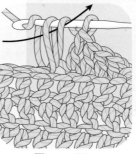

Figure 15

Figure 16

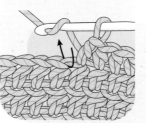

Figure 17

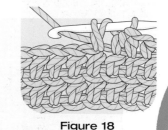

Figure 18

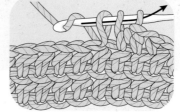

Figure 19

Treble Crochet

Treble crochet (tr) is taller than double crochet.

1. Bring the yarn over the hook twice (figure 20) and insert the hook into the next stitch.

2. Yarn over and pull the yarn through the stitch. You'll have four loops on the hook (figure 21).

3. Yarn over and pull the yarn through the first two loops (figure 22).

4. Yarn over and pull the yarn through the next two loops on the hook (figure 23).

5. Yarn over the hook and pull the yarn through the last two loops on the hook (figure 24). You've completed one treble crochet stitch. One loop remains on the hook.

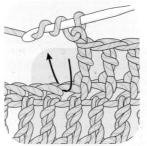

Figure 20

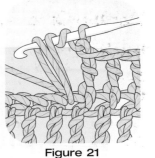

Figure 21

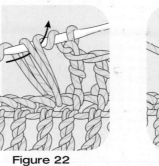

Figure 22

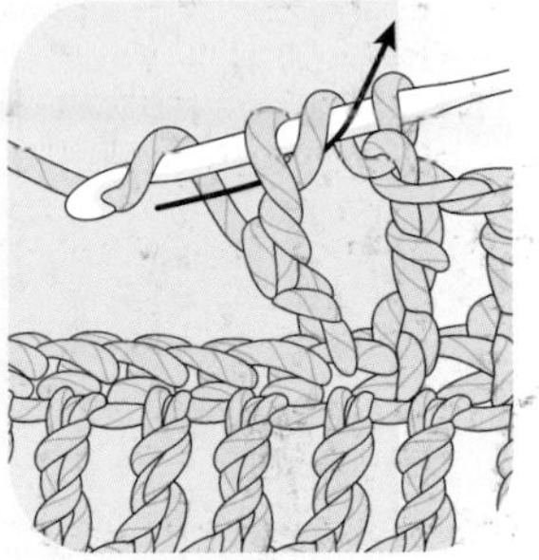

Figure 23

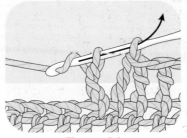

Figure 24

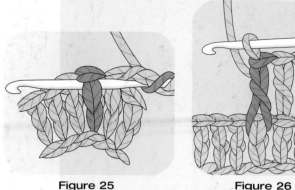

Figure 25

Figure 26

Figure 27

Figure 28

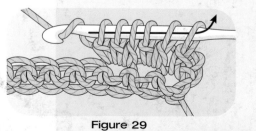

Figure 29

Front Post Double Crochet

Front post double crochet (FPdc) is a version of double crochet that is worked around the body of the stitch in the row below, instead of through the loops at the top of the next stitch.

1. Bring the yarn over the hook and insert the hook from the front around the post of a double crochet in the previous row, and through to the front again on the other side of the double crochet stitch (figure 25).

2. Yarn over and pull up a loop.

3. Yarn over and pull the yarn through two loops on the hook. Two loops remain on the hook.

4. Yarn over and pull the yarn through the last two loops on the hook. You've completed one front post double crochet. One loop remains on the hook (figure 26).

Bobble

Bobbles are used to make the thumbs and toes on some of the dolls. These instructions are for a basic double crochet bobble. Each pattern that uses a bobble includes instructions for the specific type of bobble used.

1. Bring the yarn over the hook and insert the hook into the indicated stitch.

2. Yarn over and pull up a loop.

3. Yarn over and pull the yarn through 2 loops (figure 27).

4. Rep steps 1–4 five more times, working into the same stitch (figure 28). For this bobble, you will have 7 loops on the hook. The number of loops varies depending on the specific type of bobble made.

5. Yarn over and pull the yarn through all of the loops on the hook (figure 29). You've completed one bobble. One loop remains on the hook.

Increases and Decreases

Increases are used to make a piece of crochet wider. Decreases are used to make a piece narrower.

Increases

To increase in crochet, simply work two stitches into the same stitch.

Invisible Decrease

A decrease combines two separate stitches into one stitch. I use an invisible decrease (invdec) most often.

1. (Insert the hook into the front loop only of the next st) twice (figure 30).

2. Yarn over and pull the yarn through both front loops.

3. Yarn and pull the yarn through both loops on the hook.

Single Crochet Decrease

A single crochet decrease joins two single crochet stitches into one. This decrease is used on fabric that is worked in rows or joined, turned rounds.

1. (Insert the hook into the next stitch and pull up a loop) twice.

2. Yarn over and pull the yarn through all the loops on the hook.

Figure 30

Tips for Making Dolls

The following tips will make crocheting the dolls easier.

Working in Rounds and Spirals

Most of the pieces for the dolls are worked in rounds, not straight rows. (See page 17 for instructions on making a ring to begin crocheting in the round.)

There are three ways to crochet in the round: spirals, joined rounds, and joined, turned rounds.

Spirals

The simplest way to work in the round is to make a continuous spiral. When you come to the end of the round, you just crochet into the first stitch of the previous round and keep going. This works best with single crochet, because the stitches are short enough to create a smooth spiral.

It's helpful to mark the beginning of the round in a spiral with a stitch marker. Otherwise, you won't easily be able to identify where one round begins or ends. The marker can be a locking stitch marker, a length of yarn, or a safety pin. When you get to the end of the round, remove the marker, work the stitch, and replace the marker into the new stitch.

Joined Rounds

Joined rounds are often used when working circular pieces using stitches that are taller than single crochet or in single crochet when the slant caused by the spiral is undesirable.

When working in joined rounds, crochet around the entire piece using the specified stitch. When you reach the end of the round, work a slip stitch into the first stitch of the previous round. Make one or more chains, as directed in the pattern, and begin the next round.

Note: I count the chain(s) at the beginning of each round as a stitch.

Joined, Turned Rounds

Sometimes when working in joined rounds, you will turn at the end of each round and work back in the opposite direction.

When working in joined, turned rounds, crochet around the entire piece using the specified stitch. When you reach the end of the round, work a slip stitch into the first stitch of the previous round. Turn the piece over, then make one or more chains, as directed in the pattern, and begin the next round, working in the opposite direction than the previous round.

Counting Rounds and Stitches

Don't assume that counting stitches is something only an amateur would do. Even crochet experts count their stitches. It's the only way to ensure that you're following a pattern exactly. It's a good idea to check your stitch count periodically, especially when the number of stitches in each row or round changes. This may seem like a hassle, but it will save you much frustration in the long run.

You already know how to count chain stitches in a foundation chain (see page 17).

Counting Rounds

After you work a few rounds of crochet, you'll notice that each round creates a noticeable ridge. Between the rows is an indentation, or valley, that clearly separates the rounds. The valleys are visible in spiral crochet, and in joined rounds. They are less visible in joined, turned rounds.

To count the rounds in a piece of crochet, lay your work on a flat surface. Count the ridges of each crochet round (figure 31).

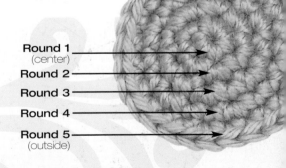

Round 1
(center)
Round 2
Round 3
Round 4
Round 5
(outside)

Figure 31

Counting Stitches

When you look even more closely at a piece of crochet, you'll see that there are several parts to each stitch.

At the top of the stitch is a V. This is where you insert your hook to work another stitch.

Along a row or round of completed stitches you will see that there are posts inside of the valleys. The posts are the vertical parts of the stitches. In between two stitches is a space, which makes up part of the valley. This is where you will insert eye shafts, when instructed in the pattern.

To count the crochet stitches in a completed row, lay your work on a flat surface. Count the vertical part—the post—of each crochet stitch as shown (figure 32).

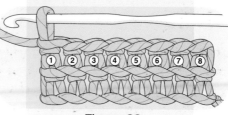

Figure 32

Closing the Hole of Remaining Stitches

When you finish working a piece of circular crochet that forms a 3-D object, you must close the small hole that remains. This is normally completed after stuffing the piece.

1. Thread the yarn tail onto a tapestry needle.

2. Insert the needle through the front loop of each stitch around the opening (figure 33).

3. Pull the tail tight to close the hole (figure 34).

4. Weave in the end and clip it close to the surface of the crochet.

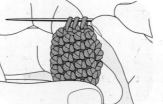
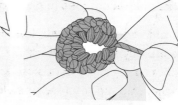

Figure 33   Figure 34

Invisible Join

When you finish working a piece of circular crochet that forms a flat circle, you must join the end of the last stitch to the first stitch of the previous round to form an invisible join.

1. Thread the yarn tail onto a tapestry needle.

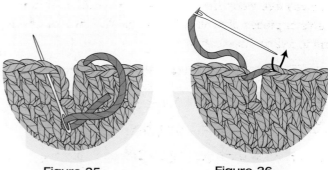

Figure 35   Figure 36

2. Pull the yarn through under the V of the first stitch of the previous round (figure 35).

3. Insert the needle into the center of the last stitch on at the end of the last round (figure 36) and pull the yarn through to secure.

4. Weave in the end and clip it close to the surface of the crochet.

Assembling your 'Gurumis

Instructions are given in the patterns telling you to "whip-stitch such and such to body using the photo as a guide," and this really is something you will have to get a feel for on your own. I define whipstiching as "sew any which way you can manage it." Some of you may well find this the most difficult part of making the dolls as it lacks the pleasant, rhythmic feel of crocheting. Don't despair; I have confidence that you will soon develop your own tricks and techniques to go along with the ones that I am about to share.

For pinning the ear, limb, tail, or whatever else I am sewing my favorite pins are the large, blunt knitting seaming pins that I mentioned in the materials section. They have heads on them that are big enough not to become lost in the crochet and the rounded tips won't split your stitches.

To do the actual stitching I use either yarn or invisible machine sewing thread. A few general rules of thumb: use yarn and a tapestry needle for pieces that are being sewn onto an area the same color as the pieces themselves or for ones that will receive more wear. Use invisible thread and a regular sewing needle for embellishments or pieces of contrasting color. When working with yarn for sewing, it is important to follow these steps:

1. Pull your yarn through the stuffed part of the amigurumi.

2. Snake it through some stitches to secure it.

3. Sew your pinned piece in place.

4 and 5. Secure the yarn again by repeating steps 2 and then 1.

6. Fasten off the yarn.

This business of snaking the yarn through some stitches is much like the process of weaving in ends. But in this case, you have three added challenges: working only from the right side, adding the length of yarn in as well as ending it off and making sure it is secure enough it attach a floppy bit.

Special Techniques

The following techniques go beyond the basics of crochet to give you skills to help make your creations unique and special.

Twisted Cord

I used a twisted cord to create the stem on the carrot on page 36. Twisted cords also make great belts and other kinds of ties.

1. Twist each strand of the cord by itself in a clockwise direction (figure 37). Do not let go, or the strands will untwist!

2. Hold all of the strands of the cord together, and let them twist onto each other in a counter clockwise direction (figure 38).

3. Tie a knot in the end of the cord to keep it from untwisting. Trim the ends even, if desired.

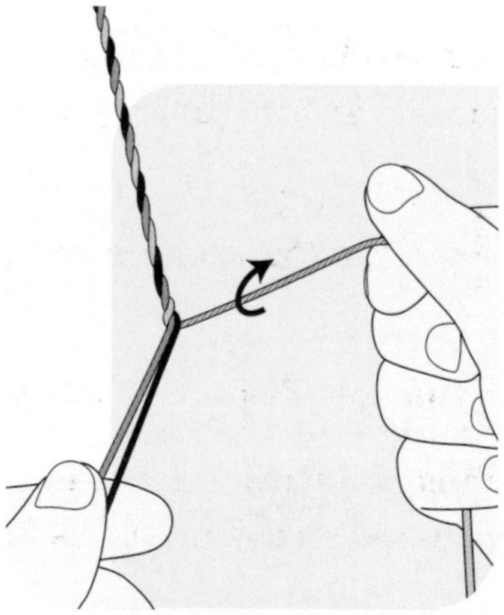

Figure 37

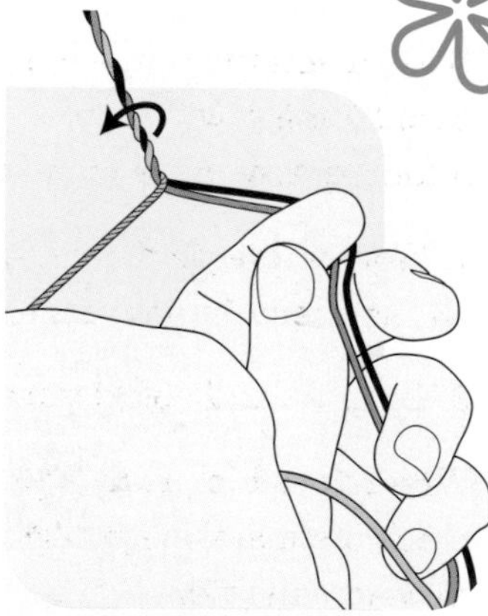

Figure 38

With the invisible thread, hiding and discreetly securing the thread is not as important. You can simply sew a knot around the post of a stitch from where you choose to start and make another knot where you stop. I do, however, like to hide the ends inside of the stuffing, if possible, because they tend to be a little pokey. While doing the whip stitching, regardless of whether or not I am using yarn or invisible thread, I prefer to go under the posts of the stitches as I feel this is the most inconspicuous, although this is not always feasible. Sometimes improvisation will be your best option.

I know this part of the process might seem like a bit of a drag, where projects tend to get stuck in the UFO (unfinished object) stage. But really that would be a shame, your are so close. The saddest sight in my studio is the "abandoned box" where unassembled doll parts languish; don't let this happen to your creations.

Stringing Beads onto Yarn

To string beads onto yarn, cut a piece of thread three or four inches (7.6 to 10.2 cm) long, fold it over a piece of yarn, and thread it onto a sewing needle as shown in figure 39. Push the thread through the bead, then pull the yarn through.

If you have trouble stringing your beads onto the yarn with a regular sewing needle, your may prefer using a flexible beading needle with a large eye (figure 40).

Seed beads are irregularly shaped and stringing them can be difficult to do if the holes in your beads are small. It's helpful to look at your beads and try to use the ones that seem to have the largest holes. If all else fails you can sew the beads on after the project is finished.

Although it's simple to remove any unused beads from the yarn after finishing your work, adding them mid-project creates extra labor, so pre-string more beads than you think you'll need.

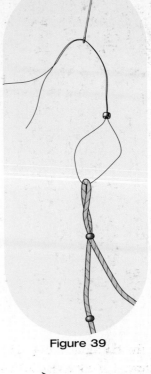

Figure 39

Changing Color (or Yarn)

Crochet might become boring if you were allowed to use only one color or one type of yarn to create a project. And imagine how difficult it would be if you had to use one—and only one—continuous thread to crochet. It would certainly make crochet a less portable craft.

Should you run out of yarn or want to change colors or yarns while you're working, avoid joining with a knot—it's messy and, incredibly, not the most secure way to attach a new piece of yarn.

1. Work to the point where there are two loops of the last stitch before the color change remaining on the hook.

2. Drop the old color; yarn over and complete the stitch with the new color.

When possible, work over the ends of the color not in use, catching them in the crochet stitches as you work the next round. This will reduce the number of ends to weave in later.

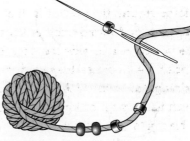

Figure 40

Taking Care of Your Hands

This tight, tight crochet can be tough on your hands. Take a break every now and then to massage and stretch your hands; see page 126 for specific exercises. Here's a testimonial haiku I wrote about the benefits of stretching.

Carpal Tunnel Stung
Wrists Hands Fingers
Ached Numb
Saved by Stretches

29

Embroidery Stitches

I use embroidery to add facial expressions and fine details to my projects. You will need an embroidery needle and perle cotton or embroidery floss to work these stitches onto the surface of a crocheted piece. If you've never done embroidery before, you may want to make a gauge circle (page 32), and practice these stitches on it before embroidering on a real project.

Blanket Stitch

This edging stitch can be decorative, functional, or both. After anchoring the thread near the fabric edge from the wrong side, insert the needle again from the right side so it's perpendicular to the fabric edge. Pass the needle over the thread and pull, repeating for each successive stitch (figure 41).

Chain Stitch

To make chain stitch, bring the needle up along the stitching line and hold the thread down with one thumb near that spot. Insert the needle right next to the point from which it emerged and bring its tip back out a short distance along the stitching line. Pull the thread through to create a loop, keeping the working thread under the needle's point. Make subsequent loops, or chains, by inserting the needle right next to the point from which it just emerged, again holding the thread down with one thumb near that spot and repeating the previous steps (figure 42).

Satin Stitch

Satin stitch is composed of parallel rows of straight stitches (figure 43).

French Knot

French knots are created by wrapping the thread around the needle one, two, or three times, then inserting it back into the fabric at the point where the needle emerged (figure 44).

Stem Stitch

In stem stitch, the thread always emerges on the left of the previous stitch. Make small, even stitches along the line to follow, sewing from left to right (figure 45).

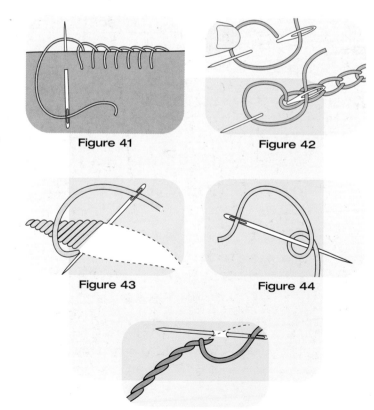

Figure 41

Figure 42

Figure 43

Figure 44

Figure 45

Abbreviations

This table lists some common crochet abbreviations.

Each pattern also includes a list of stitches and techniques used, with their abbreviations.

()	repeat the instructions in the parentheses the number of times specified		mr	make ring
			oz	ounce(s)
*	repeat the instructions after the * as instructed		patt	pattern
			RS	right side(s)
approx	approximately		rem	remain(ing)
beg	begin(ning)		rep	repeat(ing)
BLO	back loop(s) only		rnd(s)	round(s)
ch(s)	chain(s)		sc	single crochet(s)
cm	centimeter(s)		sc2tog	single crochet 2 together
dc	double crochet(s)		sk	skip
dec	decrease(-ing)		sl st	slip stitch(es)
FLO	front loop(s) only		st(s)	stitch(es)
FPdc	front post double crochet		tog	together
g	gram(s)		tr	treble crochet(s), (sometimes called triple crochet)
hdc	half double crochet(s)			
inc	increase		WS	wrong side(s)
invdec	invisible decrease		yd	yard(s)
lp(s)	loop(s)		YO	yarn over hook
m	meter(s)			

Gauge

Common knowledge would have it that gauge is not important when making stuffed toys. When I taught my first amigurumi class I had my students plunge headlong into following the pattern with no regard for gauge, with discouraging results later on. I can hear the groans from the audience already, but the fact is, as with most other knitting and crocheting patterns, gauge is important here as well. While it's true that your finished item need not fit a person's measurements, there are other, equally important reasons to make the simple gauge circle that I have provided instructions for. For one thing, in my experience, crocheters vary greatly in stitch tension. So if I use a 3.5mm/E-4 hook to make my dolls, there's no telling what size you'll need to even come close to achieving similar results.

The reason we want a specific gauge is twofold. Firstly, we want the fabric to stuff firmly and as easily as possible. As I mentioned before, stuffing can be tricky, but it is much easier to do if you take time to get the correct gauge. Stuffing a doll that has been made too loosely is endlessly frustrating. The fabric starts to pull apart and you can see the stuffing from the little holes in between the stitches. Secondly, the embellishments and templates I have provided are sized to a doll that has been made to the proper gauge, so if your doll is way too big or way too small, the eyes and other fancy bits simply will not look right.

The good news is that your gauge does not have to be super precise and you only need to measure it once for the whole book, yea! So following is a pattern for a simple circle. If you make it with a 3.5mm/E-4 hook and it is the size it should be, great. Thereafter, you can use the size hooks suggested throughout the book. But if the circle is too small, go up a hook size until your circle is the right measurement and when a pattern you're working on calls for a hook size other than 3.5mm/E-4, try going up the same amount of sizes that you went up for the gauge circle. Similarly, if your circle is too big, go down a hook size until your circle is the right measurement. When a pattern you're working on calls for a hook size other than 3.5mm/E-4, try going down the same amount of sizes that you went down for the gauge circle.

2"

Universal Gauge Circle

To make a gauge circle, you will need approx 10yd/9.1m of worsted weight "soft-type" yarn in any color, a 3.5mm/E-4 crochet hook, and a ruler.

Note: The Universal Gauge Circle is worked in joined rnds. Ch 1 at beginning of rnds counts as a stitch.

Make a starting ring (see page 17 for instructions).

Rnd 1: Ch 1, work 5 sc in ring; join with sl st in first sc; pull starting ring closed—6 sc.

Rnd 2: Ch 1, sc in first st, 2 sc in next 5 sts; join with sl st in first sc—12 sc.

Rnds 3–5: Ch 1, sc around increasing 6 sc evenly spaced around. Avoid placing increases in the same place every round; join with sl st in first sc—30 sc at end of rnd 5.

Measure across the center of the circle. The diameter of your circle should be approximately 2"/5 cm.

If your circle is too small, try again with a larger hook.

If your circle is too large, try again with a smaller hook.

Although quite similar, these brands of acrylic yarn vary slightly from each other in thickness, as do some colors within each brand. A variation of up to ⅛"/3mm should be OK.

Tasty Tidbits

Whet your appetite—crochet some food! Crocheted food is hot, even if the finished products are only room temp. Soft, stuffed food in any medium is popular right now, come to think of it—in felt, fleece, and knitting, just to name a few. Stuffed sushi is a particularly popular subject. And donuts. And mushrooms.

Why the food obsession? Maybe it's because dieting is also hot. Maybe there are so many of us going around food deprived that the only way we can start to satisfy our cravings is to make a cheeseburger out of yarn and gaze at it longingly. Gee, that theory is kind of a bummer. Perhaps it's because our brains are programmed to find food so darned great, we think it's aesthetically appealing enough to want to make tiny little food-shaped soft sculptures. Maybe that's it. Maybe it isn't accurate to label it a fad. I mean, painters have been faithfully re-creating fabulous spreads with apples, grapes, suckling pigs, roast goose, milk, and cake in still lifes for centuries now. So maybe stuffed food is just the newest manifestation of a subject matter that has always been present in art.

Whatever the reason, there is something irresistibly tempting about hooking some sensational snacks. I've arranged the projects in this chapter in order of difficulty, so if you're new to crochet these projects are the perfect size to build your confidence and your taste buds for more amigurumi. If you're already experienced? Well, I had fun making them, so I think you will too.

Not-So-Crunchy Carrot

This is a very straightforward pattern. It's fun to make because of the simple details that make it look realistic. The root is embellished with embroidered lines and the twisted cord stem requires no crochet techniques whatsoever. For those wanting to build their skills for the larger projects at the back of the book, the small circumference of the circle is great practice for making arms for the Humanoids on pages 86 to 125.

Instructions

Starting at bottom, with color A, mr.

Rnd 1: Ch 1, 4 sc in ring, pull starting ring closed (4 sc).

Rnds 2 and 3: Inc 2 sc evenly (8 sc at the end of rnd 3).

Rnd 4: Sc in each sc.

Rnd 5: Inc 1 sc (9 sc).

Rnd 6: Sc in each sc.

Rnds 7–24: Rep rnds 5 and 6 nine times (18 sts).

Rnd 25: (Invdec, sc in the next st) 6 times (12 sts).

Switch to color B in last st of rnd 25.

Rnd 26: (Invdec, sc in the next 2 sts) 3 times (9 sts).

Finishing

Stuff carrot. Fasten off, leaving an 18"/45.7cm tail. Thread onto tapestry needle. Close the hole as illustrated on page 26. Bring the yarn end up through the center of the hole. Cut an additional 18"/45.7cm length of color B. With tapestry needle, thread it under rnd 26 leaving 9"/22.9cm on either side. Make a twisted cord (see page 28 for instructions) with these three lengths of yarn for the carrot stem. Knot the end of the cord with an overhand knot. If desired, use Perle cotton and an embroidery needle to add chain stitch embroidery on carrot as shown in the photo.

April 18

Decisions, Decisions

I think carrots must come in different carrot-y flavors, because the first bunny I gave one to had a sweet, innocent expression and the next bunny that got a carrot had a grumpy, sour look. Bunnies can be kinda picky, though—this one can't decide whether he likes these carrots or not.

Fresh Strawberries

A pint of these life-sized crocheted berries would look sweet displayed in a basket or bowl. The Humanoids like to carry them around as snacks, too. Just sew a loop of elastic onto the back of the berry that's small enough to fit tightly around their little hands.

May 2

No Way. Never Again.

The first strawberry I made had very carefully embroidered seeds that were light green with yellow accents in the middle. It took a lot of time, a lot of work, and a lot of junk food. I finally decided that went in the category of insane perfectionism and used beads the next time instead.

Skill Level
Easy

Finished Measurements
Approx 2"/5.1cm tall by 1¼"/3.2cm wide

You Will Need
Worsted weight "soft-type" acrylic yarn in red
See page 10 for tips on estimating yarn amounts.
Crochet hook:
   3.5mm/E-4 or size to obtain gauge
Polyester fiberfill
Tapestry needle
Wool or wool-blend felt, green
Perle cotton, size 5, light green
Embroidery needle
Craft glue
Straight pins
Invisible thread
Beading needle
50 pale yellow seed beads, size 10
Template, page 127

Gauge
5 rnd gauge circle = 2"/5cm
See page 32 for instructions on making a gauge circle.

Stitches and Techniques Used
Make ring (mr), page 17
Single crochet (sc)
Invisible decrease (invdec), page 23
Blanket stitch, page 30
Satin stitch, page 30
French knot, page 30

Instructions

Starting at bottom, mr.

Rnd 1: Ch 1, 4 sc in ring, pull starting ring closed (4 sc).

Rnd 2: Inc 2 sc evenly spaced (6 sc).

Rnd 3: Inc 3 sc evenly spaced (9 sc).

Rnd 4: Sc in each sc.

Rnds 5 and 6: Rep rnds 3 and 4 (12 sc at end of rnd 6).

Rnds 7–10: Inc 3 sc evenly (24 sc after rnd 10).

Rnd 11: Sc in each sc.

Rnd 12: (Invdec, sc in the next 2 st) 6 times (18 sts).

Rnd 13: (Sc in the next st, invdec) 6 times (12 sts).

Rnd 14: (Invdec, sc in the next 2 st) 3 times (9 sts).

Finishing

Stuff berry. Fasten off, leaving an 18"/45.7cm tail. Thread tail onto tapestry needle. Close hole as illustrated on page 26. Weave in end.

Strawberry Hull

Cut one star shape out of green felt, using the template on page 127 as a guide.

Using the light green Perle cotton and embroidery needle, work blanket stitch around the edge of the hull. Work a satin-stitch star in the middle of the hull, referring to the photo as a guide. In the middle of the satin-stitched star, embroider one French knot.

Glue the hull to the top of the strawberry using straight pins to keep it in place while it dries.

Seeds

With invisible thread and beading needle, sew approx 50 seed beads all over the strawberry, spacing them randomly. Try to nestle the beads into the valleys in between the rnds so they look more realistic. (See page 25 for instructions.)

This project was made with 1 skein of
Red Heart's Soft (100% acrylic, 5oz/140g, approx 256yd/234m) in #5142, Cherry Red

Sandwich Cookie

Only the grumpiest of grumps wouldn't find a plateful of these tasty treats amusing. Secret: the cookie half is also a darling flower. Make it on its own in fancy yarn scraps for a cute pin or embellishment.

Instructions

Cookie (make 2)

Note: Cookie is worked in joined rnds. Ch 1 at beginning of rnds counts as a st.

Starting at bottom, with color A, mr.

Rnd 1: Ch 1, 5 sc in ring, sl st to first sc to join, pull starting ring closed (6 sc).

Rnd 2: Ch 1, sc in the same sp, 2 sc in the next 5 sc, sl st to first sc to join (12 sc).

Rnd 3: Ch 1, sc in the same sp, sc in the next st, (2 sc in the next st, sc in the next st) 5 times, sl st to first sc to join (18 cs).

Rnd 4: Ch 3, sk the sp you sl st-ed into and the next st, sc in the next st, (ch 2, sk the next st, sc in the next st) 6 times, ch 2, sl st into the first ch of the rnd (9 ch 2 lps).

Rnd 5: Ch 1, [(sc 3 hdc sc) in the next ch 2 loop, sk next sc] 9 times.

Fasten off, leaving an 18"/45.7cm tail. Join to first sc of rnd 5 as illustrated on page 26. Weave in ends.

Crème Filling (make 1)

Note: Filling is worked in a continuous spiral. Do not join rnds. You may wish to use a marker to indicate the beginning of the rnd.

Starting at bottom, with color B, mr.

Rnd 1: Ch 1, 6 sc in ring, pull starting ring closed (6 sc).

Rnd 2: 2 sc in each st (12 sc).

Rnds 3–6: Inc 6 sc evenly spaced (36 sc at the end of rnd 6).

Rnd 7: Sc in each sc.

Skill Level
Easy

Finished Measurements
Approx 2"/5.1cm diameter

You Will Need
Worsted weight "soft-type" acrylic yarn:
    Color A: brown
    Color B: off white
See page 10 for tips on estimating yarn amounts.
Crochet hook:
    3.5mm/E-4 *or size to obtain gauge*
Tapestry needle

Gauge
5 rnd gauge circle = 2"/5cm
See page 32 for instructions on making a gauge circle.

Stitches and Techniques Used
Make ring (mr), page 17
Chain (ch)
Single crochet (sc)
Slip stitch (sl st)
Skip (sk)
Half double crochet (hdc)
Invisible decrease (invdec), page 23
Repeat (rep)

Rnd 8: (Invdec, sc in the next 4 st) 6 times (30 sts).

Rnd 9: Sc in the next 2 sts, (invdec, sc in the next 3 sts) 5 times, invdec, sc in the next st (24 sts).

Rnd 10: (Invdec, sc in the next 2 st) 6 times (18 sts).

Rnd 11: (Sc in the next st, invdec) 6 times (12 sts).

Rnd 12: (Invdec, sc in the next 2 st) 3 times (9 sts).

Fasten off, leaving an 18"/45.7cm tail. Close hole as illustrated on page 26. Weave in end.

Assembly

Flatten crème filling. Stack cookies on either side of filling with WS facing in. Using the tapestry needle and an 18"/45.7cm length of A, sew all three pieces together through rnd 3 of the cookies; there is no need to sew the petals down. Weave in ends.

This project was made with 1 skein each of

Color A: Bernat's Satin (100% acrylic, 3.5oz/100g, 166yd/152m), in #040130, Mocha

Color B: Bernat's Satin (100% acrylic, 3.5oz/100g, 166yd/152m), in #04007, Silk

March 25

Sugar and Spice and Everything Nice

When I was a little girl, tea parties were some of my favorite playtimes. Normally, I'm not a sentimental person, but someday I want to crochet a tea set and these cookies would be a very nice addition.

My crocheted cupcakes would be perfect with a tea set, too. Don't pretty cupcakes just make you smile? I'm way better at crocheting than I am at baking, plus sweets aren't really my thing. Voilà, the perfect solution! And they're non-perishable, too.

Cutecakes

These crocheted confections would make adorable zipper pulls or cell phone charms if you attached a lobster claw clasp to the top. They would also be a welcome addition to any little girl's tea party set.

Skill Level

Intermediate

Finished Measurements

Approx 2"/5.1cm tall by 1½"/3.8cm wide

You Will Need

Worsted weight "soft-type" acrylic yarn:
  Color A: pink
  Color B: chocolate brown
  Color C: lime green
See page 10 for tips on estimating your amounts.
Crochet hooks:
  3.5mm/E-4 *or size to obtain gauge*
  3.25mm/D-3
  2.75 mm/C-2
Polyester fiberfill
Tapestry needle
Invisible thread
Beading needle
40 pink seed beads, size 10

Gauge

5 rnd gauge circle = 2"/5cm
See page 32 for instructions on making a gauge circle.

Stitches and Techniques Used

Make ring (mr), page 17
Single crochet (sc)
Crab stitch (reverse single crochet)
Front Loop Only (FLO)
Back Loop Only (BLO)
Invisible decrease (invdec), page 23
Front Post Double Crochet (FPdc)

Instructions

Cutecake Top (make 1)

Starting at icing, with 3.5mm/E-4 hook and color A, mr.

Note: Cutecake Top is worked in a continuous spiral. Do not join rnds except as noted. You may wish to use a marker to indicate the beginning of the rnd.

Rnd 1: Ch 1, 6 sc in ring, pull starting ring closed (6 sc).

Rnd 2: Inc in each sc (12 sc).

Rnds 3 and 4: Inc 3 sc evenly spaced (18 sc at the end of rnd 4).

Rnd 5: Sc in each sc.

Rnd 6: Sc in each sc. Join to second sc in rnd with a sl st. Ch 1. Do not turn.

Rnd 7: Work crab stitch in FLO. Fasten off color A. Weave in end.

Rnd 8: Attach color B in any back loop. Working in BLO, sc in each st. Do not join.

Rnd 9: Sc in each st, working through both loops.

Rnd 10: Invdec 9 times (9 sts).

Stuff cutecake top.

Fasten off, leaving an 18"/45.7cm tail. Thread tail onto tapestry needle. Close hole as illustrated on page 26. Weave in end.

Paper (make 1)

Starting at bottom, with 3.25mm/D-3 hook and color C, mr.

Note: Paper is worked in joined rnds. Starting ch at beginning of rnds counts as a stitch.

Rnd 1: Ch 1, 5 sc in ring, join with sl st in first sc, pull starting ring closed (6 sc).

Rnd 2: Ch 1, sc in same sc as join, 2 sc in next 5 st join with sl st in first sc (12 sc).

Switch to 2.75mm/C-2 hook.

Rnd 3: Ch 3, dc in each st, join with sl st in first dc.

Rnds 4 and 5: Ch3, work in FPdc and inc 3 sts evenly spaced, join with sl st in first dc (18 sts at the end of rnd 5).

Fasten off. Weave in end.

Finishing

Using invisible thread, sew paper to cutecake top, stuffing the paper if it seems like it needs it.

With invisible thread and beading needle sew approx 40 seed beads sprinkled on top of icing. Try to nestle the beads into the valleys in between the rnds. (See instructions on page 25.)

This project was made with 1 skein each of

Color A: Caron's Simply Soft (100% acrylic, 3oz/85g, 165yd/151m), in #2614, Soft Pink

Color B: Bernat's Satin (100% acrylic, 3.5oz/100g, 166yd/152m), in #040130, Mocha

Color C: Caron's Simply Soft Brites (100% acrylic, 3oz/85g, 165yd/151m), in #9607, Limelight

Cheeseburger with the Works

Many of the designs in this book existed prior to its writing. Not the cheeseburger. A bright, pop-icon of a crocheted sandwich had been a thought in the back of my mind for a while, and then the opportunity arose with this chapter. Do you want fries with that?

Skill Level
Intermediate

Finished Measurements
Bun: 3"/7.6cm diameter
Lettuce: 4"/10.2cm diameter
Onions: 2½"/6.4cm diameter
Tomatoes: 2"/5.1cm diameter
Hamburger patty: 3"/7.6cm diameter

You Will Need
Worsted weight "soft-type" acrylic
   yarn:
   Color A: brown
   Color B: copper
   Color C: green
   Color D: pale gold
   Color E: pale orange
   Color F: orchid
   Color G: red
   Color H: red-violet
*See page 10 for tips on estimating
   yarn amounts.*
Crochet hooks:
   3.5mm/E-4 *or size to obtain gauge*
   3.25mm/D-3
Tapestry needle
Invisible thread
Sewing needle

Gauge
5 rnd gauge circle = 2"/5cm
*See page 32 for instructions on mak-
   ing a gauge circle.*

Stitches and Techniques Used
Make ring (mr), page 17
Chain (ch)
Ch sp (chain space)
Single crochet (sc)
Invisible decrease (invdec), page 23
Slip stitch (sl st)
Half double crochet (hdc)
Skip (sk)
Treble crochet (tr)
Changing colors,
   page 29

July 18

(Pop) Art Imitates Life

It's hard to believe that this greasy thing could be inspiring, but….I studied painting in college and have always loved pop art the best. That being said, I can't help but think of my cheeseburger as a tiny offspring of Claes Oldenburg's *Floor Burger*, a gigantic stuffed fast-food sandwich.

Instructions

Patty (make 1)

Note: Patty is worked in a continuous spiral. Do not join rnds. You may wish to use a marker to indicate the beginning of the rnd.

Starting at bottom, with 3.5mm/E-4 hook and color A, mr.

Rnd 1: Ch 1, 6 sc in ring (6 sc).

Rnd 2: 2 sc in each sc (12 sc).

Rnds 3–8: Inc 6 sc evenly spaced (48 sc at the end of rnd 8).

Rnd 9: Sc in each st.

Rnd 10: (Invdec, sc in the next 6 sts) 6 times (42 sts).

Rnd 11: Sc in the next 2 sts, (invdec, sc in the next 5 sts) 5 times, invdec over the next 2 st, sc in the next 3 sts (36 sts).

Rnd 12: (Sc in the next 4 sts, invdec) 6 times (30 sts).

Rnd 13: Sc in the next 2 sts, (invdec, sc in the next 3 sts) 5 times, invdec over the next 2 sts, sc in the next st (24 sts).

Rnd 14: (Invdec, sc in the next 2 sts) 6 times (18 sts).

Rnd 15: (Sc in the next st, invdec) 6 times (12 sts).

Rnd 16: (Invdec, sc in the next 2 sts) 3 times (9 sts).

Fasten off, leaving an 18"/45.7cm tail. Thread tail onto tapestry needle. Close hole as illustrated on page 26. Weave in end. Flatten patty so it will fit in bun.

Cheese (make 1)

Note: Cheese is worked in joined, turned rounds. Ch 1 at beginning of rnds counts as a stitch. This technique may seem difficult at first as it is a bit of a change, but with practice you will adapt to it easily.

Starting in center, with 3.5mm/E-4 hook and color E, mr.

Rnd 1 (right side): Ch 1, work 5 sc in ring; join with sl st in first sc; pull starting ring closed (6 sc).

Rnd 2 (wrong side): Ch 1, turn, sc in first st, 2 sc in next 5 sts; join with sl st in first sc (12 sc).

Rnd 3: Ch 1, turn, sc in next sc, *(sc, hdc, sc) in next sc, sc in next 2 sc; rep from * 2 more times, (sc, hdc, sc) in last sc; sc in last; join with sl st in first sc (20 sts).

Rnd 4: Ch 1, turn, sc in next 2 sts, *(sc, hdc, sc) in next st, sc in next 4 sts; rep from * 2 more times, (sc, hdc, sc) in next st, sc in last st; join with sl st in first sc (28 sts).

Rnd 5: Ch 1, turn, sc in next 3 sts, *(sc, hdc, sc) in next st, sc in next 6 sts; rep from * 2 more times, (sc, hdc, sc) in next st, sc in last 2 sts; join with sl st in first sc (36 sts).

Rnd 6: Ch 1, turn, sc in next 4 sts, *(sc, hdc, sc) in next st, sc in next 8 sts; rep from * 2 more times, (sc, hdc, sc) in next st, sc in last 3 sts; join with sl st in first sc (44 sts).

Rnd 7: Ch 1, turn, sc in next 5 sts, *(sc, hdc, sc) in next st, sc in next 10 sts; rep from * 2 more times, (sc, hdc, sc) in next st, sc in last 4 sts; join with sl st in first sc (52 sts).

Rnd 8: Ch 1, turn, sc in next 6 sts, *(sc, hdc, sc) in next st, sc in next 12 sts; rep from * 2 more times, (sc, hdc, sc) in next st, sc in last 5 sts; do not sl st to join (60 sts).

Fasten off, leaving an 18"/45.7cm tail. Join as illustrated on page 26. Weave in ends.

Lettuce (make 1)

Note: Lettuce is worked in a continuous spiral. Do not join rnds. You may wish to use a marker to indicate the beginning of the rnd.

Starting in center, with 3.5mm/E-4 hook and color C, mr.

Rnd 1: Ch 1, work 6 sc in ring, pull starting ring closed (6 sc).

Rnd 2: 2 sc in each st (12 sc).

Rnds 3–6: Inc 6 sc evenly spaced (36 sc at the end of rnd 6).

Rnd 8: Ch 8 (counts as 1 tr plus ch 3), (sk 2 st, tr in the next st, ch 3) 11 times, sk 2 sts, sl st to ch 3 of beginning ch to join (12 ch sp).

Rnd 9: Ch 4, 7 tr around the ch 3 post at the beginning of rnd 8, sc in the next ch sp, (8 tr around the post of the next tr from rnd 8, sc in the next ch sp) 11 times.

Fasten off, leaving an 18"/45.7cm tail. Join to first ch at beginning of rnd 9 as illustrated on page 26. Weave in ends.

Tomato (make 2)

Note: Tomato is worked in joined rounds. Ch 1 at beginning of rnds counts as a stitch.

Starting at center, with 3.5mm/E-4 hook and color G, mr.

Rnd 1: Ch 1, 7 sc in ring, sl st to first sc to join (8 sc).

Rnd 2: Ch 1, sc in the same sp, 2 sc in the next 7 sc, sl st to first sc to join (16 sc).

Rnd 3: Ch 4 (counts as 1 hdc plus ch 2), sk the sp you slst-ed in to and the next st, hdc in the next st, (ch 2, sk the next st, hdc in the next st) 6 times, ch 2, sk the last st, sl st into 2nd ch at beginning of rnd (8 ch sp).

Rnd 4: Ch 1, 3 sc in the next ch sp, (sk the next hdc, 4 sc in the next ch sp) 7 times (32 sts).

Fasten off, leaving an 18"/45.7cm tail. Join to first sc of rnd 4 as illustrated on page 26. Weave in ends.

Red Onion Slice (make 2)

Note: Onion slices are worked in joined rnds. Ch 1 at beginning of rnds counts as a stitch.

Rnd 1: With 3.5mm/E-4 hook and color F, ch 29. Sl st to first ch to form a ring being careful not to twist (30 sts, sl st counts as a st).

Rnd 2: Ch 1, sc in the same sp, sc in the next 4 sts, (2 sc in the next st, sc in the next 4 st) 5 times (36 sc).

Rnd 3: Change to color H. Inc 6 sc evenly spaced (42 sc).

Fasten off, leaving an 18"/45.7cm tail. Join to first sc of rnd 3 as illustrated on page 26. Weave in ends.

Top Half of Bun (make 1)

Note: Bun is worked in a continuous spiral. Do not join rnds. You may wish to use a marker to indicate the beginning of the rnd.

Starting at bottom, with 3.5mm/E-4 hook and color B, mr.

Rnd 1: Ch 1, 6 sc in ring (6 sc).

Rnd 2: Ch 1, 2 sc in each st (12 sc).

Rnd 3-6: Inc 6 sc evenly spaced (36 sc at the end of rnd 6).

Rnd 7-12: Inc 3 sc evenly spaced (54 sc at the end of rnd 13).

Rnd 11: Switch to color E. Sc in each st.

Switch to 3.25mm/D 3 hook.

Rnd 12: (Sc in the next 7 st, invdec) 6 times (48 sts).

Rnd 13: Sc in the next 2 sts, (invdec, sc in the next 6 sts) 5 times, invdec, sc in the next 4 sts (42 sts).

Rnd 14: (Sc in the next 5 sts, invdec) 6 times (36 sts).

Rnd 15: Sc in the next 2 sts, (invdec, sc in the next 4 sts) 5 times, invdec, sc in the next 2 sts (30 sts).

Rnd 16: (Sc in the next 3 sts, invdec) 6 times (24 sts).

Rnd 17: (Invdec, sc in the next 2 sts) 6 times (18 sts).

Rnd 18: (Sc in the next st, invdec) 6 times (12 sts).

Rnd 19: (Invdec, sc in the next 2 sts) 3 times (9 sts).

Fasten off, leaving an 18"/45.7cm tail. Stuff top half of bun lightly. Close hole as illustrated on page 26. Weave in end.

Bottom Half of Bun (make 1)

Note: Bun is worked in a continuous spiral. Do not join rnds. You may wish to use a marker to indicate the beginning of the rnd.

Starting at bottom, with 3.5mm/E-4 hook and color B, mr.

Rnd 1: Ch 1, 6 sc in ring (6 sc).

Rnd 2: Ch 1, 2 sc in each st (12 sc).

Rnds 3–8: Inc 6 sc evenly spaced (48 sc at the end of rnd 8).

Rnds 9 and 10: Inc 3 sc evenly spaced (54 sc at the end of rnd 9).

Rnd 11: Switch to color E. Sc in each sc.

Switch to 3.25mm/D-3 hook.

Rnd 12: (Sc in the next 7 st, invdec) 6 times (48 sts).

Rnd 13: Sc in the next 2 sts, (invdec, sc in the next 6 sts) 5 times, invdec, sc in the next 4 sts (42 sts).

Rnd 14: (Sc in the next 5 sts, invdec) 6 times (36 sts).

Rnd 15: Sc in the next 2 sts, (invdec, sc in the next 4 sts) 5 times, invdec, sc in the next 2 sts (30 sts).

Rnd 16: (Sc in the next 3 st, invdec) 6 times (24 sts).

Rnd 17: (Invdec, sc in the next 2 st) 6 times (18 sts).

Rnd 18: (Sc in the next st, invdec) 6 times (12 sts).

Rnd 19: (Invdec, sc in the next 2 st) 3 times (9 sts).

Fasten off, leaving an 18"/45.7cm tail. Stuff bottom half of bun lightly. Close hole as illustrated on page 26. Weave in end.

This project was made with 1 skein each of

Color A: Bernat's Satin (100% acrylic, 3.5oz/100g, 166yd/152m), in #040130, Mocha

Color B: Caron's Simply Soft (100% acrylic, 3.5oz/100g, 166yd/152m), in #2714, Copper Kettle

Color C: Bernat's Satin (100% acrylic, 3.5oz/100g, 166yd/152m), in #04712, Palm

Color D: Caron's Simply Soft (100% acrylic, 3.5oz/100g, 166yd/152m), in #2713, Buttercup

Color E: Caron's Simply Soft Brites (100% acrylic, 3.5oz/100g, 166yd/152m), in #2605, Mango

Color F: Bernat's Satin (100% acrylic, 3.5oz/100g, 166yd/152m), in #04420, Sea Shell

Color G: Red Heart's Soft (100% acrylic, 5 oz/140g, 256 yd/234m), in #5142, Cherry Red

Color H: Bernat's Satin (100% acrylic, 3.5oz/100g, 166yd/152m), in #04732, Maitai

Skelly Fish

Flimsy, floppy
crocheted fish bones.
Silly I know, but fun.

October 6

Look Within

Towards the end of the book-writing process I was visiting my favorite photo-sharing website for some inspiration, when I happened upon a photo of a whimsical piece of graffiti. It was a very Dr. Seuss-like dead fish, perfect! I knew then that I had my final pattern. Sometimes what's inside (the skeleton) is more interesting than what's outside (lunch).

Skill Level
Intermediate

Finished Measurements
Approx 10"/25.4cm long

You Will Need
Worsted weight "soft-type" acrylic
  yarn:
  Color A: bright pink
  Color B: pink
  Color C: avocado
  Color D: cream
*See page 10 for tips on estimating
  yarn amounts.*
Crochet hooks:
  3.5mm/E-4 *or size to obtain gauge*
  3.25 mm /D-3
Polyester fiberfill
Tapestry needle
Perle cotton, size 5, or embroidery
  floss, black
Embroidery needle
Invisible thread
Sewing needle

Gauge
5 rnd gauge circle = 2"/5cm
*See page 32 for instructions on mak-
  ing a gauge circle.*

Stitches and Techniques Used
Single crochet (sc)
Slip stitch (sl st)
Changing colors, page 29
Invisible decrease (invdec), page 23
Make ring (mr)

Instructions

Fish Head (make 1)

Note: Fish head is worked in joined, oval rnds. Ch 1 does not count as a stitch in this piece.

With 3.25mm/D-3 hook and color A, ch 9.

Rnd 1: Working in back bumps of foundation ch, 2 sc in second ch from hook, sc in next 6 ch, 3 sc in last ch; working along opposite side of beginning ch, sc in next 6 ch; join with sl st in first sc (18 sts).

Rnd 2: Ch 1, sc in same st as join, 2 sc in next 2 st, sc in next 6 sts, 2 sc in next 3 st, sc in next 6 sts, join with sl st in first sc (24 sts).

Change to color B.

Rnd 3: Ch 1, 2 sc in same st as join, sc in next st, (2 sc in next st, sc in next st) 2 times, sc in next 6 sts, (2 sc in next st, sc in next st) 3 times, sc in next 5 sts, join with sl st in first sc (30 sts).

Rnd 4: Ch 1, sc in same st as join, sc in next st, 2 sc in next st, (sc in next 2 st, 2 sc in next st) 2 times, sc in next 6 sts, (sc in next 2 st, 2 sc in next st) 3 times, sc in next 5 sts, join with sl st in first sc (36 sts).

Change to color C and 3.5mm/E-4 hook

Rnds 5 and 6: Ch 1, sc in each sc around, join with sl st in first sc.

Rnd 7: Ch 1, sc in same st as join, sc in next st, invdec, (sc in next 2 st, invdec) 2 times, sc in next 6 sts, (sc in next 2 st, invdec) 3 times, sc in next 5 sts, join with sl st in first sc (30 sts).

Rnds 8 and 9: Ch 1, sc in each sc around, join with sl st in first sc.

Rnd 10: Ch 1, invdec over same st as join and next st, sc in next st, (invdec, sc in next st) 2 times, sc in next 6 sts, (invdec, sc in next st) 3 times, sc in next 5 sts, join with sl st in first sc (24 sts).

Rnd 11: Ch 1, sc in each sc around, join with sl st in first sc.

Rnd 12: Ch 1, invdec over same st as join and next st, (invdec) 2 times, sc in next 6 sts, (invdec) 3 times, sc in next 5 sts, join with sl st in first sc (18 sts).

Rnd 13: Ch 1, sc in each sc around, join with sl st in first sc.

Rnds 14–16: Ch 1, sc in each sc around, invdec 3 times evenly spaced around, join with sl st in first (9 sts).

Fasten off, leaving an 18"/45.7cm tail. Stuff head. Close hole as illustrated on page 26. Weave in ends. Using two 12"/30.5cm strands of Perle cotton, embroider an X for the eye on each side of the head.

Mouth (make 1)

Note: Mouth is worked in a continuous spiral. Do not join rnds. You may wish to use a marker to indicate the beginning of the rnd.

With 3.5mm/E-4 hook and color A, mr.

Rnd 1: Ch 1, 4 sc in ring, pull starting ring closed (4 sts).

Rnds 2–5: Inc 2 sc evenly spaced (12 sts at the end of rnd 5).

Rnds 6 and 7: Sc in each sc around.

Fasten off, leaving an 18"/45.7cm tail. Use tail to sew mouth to head using photo as a guide. Weave in ends.

Skeleton (make 1)

With 3.25mm/E-4 hook and color D, ch 34.

Rnd 1: Working in back bumps of foundation, sc in second ch from hook, sc in next 3 ch, ch 7, sl st in second ch from hook, sc in next 10 ch, ch 6, sl st in second ch from hook, sc in next 9 ch, ch 5, sl st in second ch from hook, sc in next 8 ch, ch 4, sl st in second ch from hook, sc in next 7 ch, ch 3, sl st in second ch from hook, sc in next 6 ch, ch 2, sl st in second ch from hook, sc in next 3 ch, 3 sc in last ch, working along opposite side of starting ch, sc in next, ch 2, sl st in second ch from hook, sc in next 5 ch, ch 3, sl st in second ch from hook, sc in next 6 ch, ch 4, sl st in second ch from hook, sc in next 7 ch, ch 5, sl st in second ch from hook, sc in next 8 ch, ch 6, sl st in second ch from hook, sc in next 9 ch, ch 7, sl st in second ch from hook, sc in next 9 ch.

Fasten off. Weave in ends. With invisible thread sew bones onto fish head using photo as a guide.

Tail Fins (make 2)

With 3.5mm/E-4 hook and color C, ch 13.

Row 1: Working in back bumps of foundation, sc in second ch from hook, sc in next 10 ch, 3 sc in last ch, working along opposite side of starting ch, sc in next 8, ch 3, turn.

Work through back loop only for remainder of fin. This makes a ribbed texture.

Row 2: Sl st in third ch from hook, sc in next 9 sc, 3 sc in next sc, sc in next 7 sc, ch 3, turn.

Rows 3 and 4: Sl st in third ch from hook, sc in next 8 sc, 3 sc in next sc, sc in next 7 sc, ch 3, turn.

Row 5: Sl st in third ch from hook, sc in next 5 sc, sl st in next 3 sc.

Fasten off. Weave in ends. Using photo as a guide, over-lap tail fins sandwiching tip of bones between them. Sew in place with invisible thread.

This project was made with 1 skein each of

Color A: Caron's Simply Soft (100% acrylic, 3oz/85g, 165yd/151m), in #2604, Watermelon

Color B: Caron's Simply Soft (100% acrylic, 3oz/85g, 165yd/151m), in #2614, Soft Pink

Color C: Red Heart's Soft (100% acrylic, 5oz/140g, approx. 256yd/234m), in #4420, Guacamole

Color D: Bernat's Satin, (100% acrylic, 3.5oz/100g, 166yd/152m), in #04007, Silk

Further Along the Food Chain

In this chapter we move up the food chain, away from Tasty Tidbits and towards more complicated creatures. Don't be intimidated by these patterns. If you made some of the edibles in the previous chapter, you're ready. The extra effort required to make these animals is well worth it. After all, a carrot can't reach the cuteness factor of a fawn or piglet. Again, these patterns are in approximate order of difficulty so if you're feeling a bit timid, try the mouse or the wiener dog first.

This is a fun chapter, one that will help you appreciate how end- lessly sculpt-able this type of crochet can be.

Mighty L'il Mouse

Something about this tiny mouse captures people's hearts. I recently made one for a preteen boy who requested one for his birthday. Imagine that! Clearly, anything is possible.

Skill Level
Easy

Finished Measurements
Approx 3"/7.6cm long

You Will Need
Worsted weight "soft-type" acrylic
 yarn in light aqua
*See page 10 for tips on estimating
 yarn amounts.*
Crochet hooks:
 3.5mm/E-4 or size to obtain gauge
 3.25mm/D-3
 2.75mm/C-2
Locking stitch marker
Invisible thread
Beading needle
2 black seed beads, size 6
Perle cotton, size 5, hot pink
Embroidery needle
Blush and cotton swabs
Tapestry needle
Polyester fiberfill
Knee-high nylon (optional)
PVC pellets (optional)

Caution: The PVC pellets listed
 above are not child-safe. If you're
 making this project for a child, use
 polyester fiberfill for stuffing.

Gauge
5 rnd gauge circle = 2"/5cm
*See page 32 for instructions on mak-
 ing a gauge circle.*

Stitches and Techniques Used
Make ring (mr), page 17
Double crochet (dc)
Slip stitch (sl st)
Single crochet (sc)
Half double crochet (hdc)
Invisible decrease (invdec), page 23

Instructions

Ears (make 2)

With 2.75mm/C-2 hook, mr.

Rnd 1: Ch 3, 6 dc in first ch, ch 2, sl st in ring, pull starting ring closed (7 sc).

Fasten off, leaving an 18"/45.7cm tail.

Mouse Body

Note: Mouse body is worked in a continuous spiral. Do not join rnds. You may wish to use a marker to indicate the beginning of the rnd.

Starting at tip of nose, with 3.25/D-3 hook, mr.

Rnd 1: Ch 1, 4 sc in ring, pull starting ring closed (4 sc).

Rnd 2: Inc 2 sc (6 sc).

Rnd 3: Inc 3 sc (9 sc).

Switch to 3.5mm/E-4 hook.

Rnd 4: Sc in each sc.

Rnd 5: (2 sc in next st, 1 sc in next st) 3 times, sc in next 3 sc (12 sc).

Rnd 6: (2 sc in next st, 1 sc in next 2 sts) 3 times, sc in next 3 sc (15 sc).

Rnd 7: (2 sc in next st, 1 sc in next 3 sts) 3 times, sc in next 3 sc (18 sc).

Rnd 8: (2 sc in next st, 1 sc in next 4 sts) 3 times, sc in next 3 sc (21 sc).

Rnd 9: (2 sc in next st, 1 sc in next 5 sts) 3 times, sc in next 3 sc (24 sc).

Rnd 10: (2 sc in next st, 1 sc in next 6 sts) 3 times, sc in next 3 sc (27 sc).

Rnd 11: (2 sc in next st, 1 sc in next 7 sts) 3 times, sc in next 3 sc (30 sc).

Rnds 12–14: (Sc in next 3 sts, hdc in next 12 sts, sc in next 15 sts) 3 times.

Rnd 15: Sc in next 3 st, hdc in next 12 st, mark as end of rnd (30 sts).

Rnd 16: Sc in each sc.

Before you proceed to rnd 17, put your working loop on a locking marker to save it for later so you can embroider the nose and otherwise embellish the small cone shape you've crocheted to make it look like a mouse. (You could also save this work for the end, but it is much easier to hide the end of your yarn and thread this way).

Referring to photo of mouse as a guide, embellish face as follows.

•**Eyes:** Using invisible thread and beading needle, sew seed beads betweens rnds 3 and 4, four posts apart on the side of the body with the hdc.

•**Nose:** Cut a 12"/30.5cm length of Perle cotton and use the embroidery needle to sew an X in the appropriate spot.

•**Ears:** Using fastened-off ends, whipstitch ears centered below eyes between rnds 5 and 6. Dab a bit of blush in the ears using the cotton swabs.

Replace working loop on hook and proceed to rnd 17.

Rnds 17–19: Invdec 6 sc evenly spaced (12 sts at end of rnd 19).

Stuff mouse, using polyester fiberfill or a combination of fiberfill and half of a knee-high nylon filled with PVC pellets if desired.

Fasten off, leaving an 18"/45.7cm tail. Close hole as illustrated on page 26. Weave in end.

Tail (make 1)

With 3.25/D-3 hook, ch 36.

Row 1: With 2.75mm/C-2 hook, sl st in 2nd ch and in each ch until 2nd to last ch, ch 1 (35 sts).

Fasten off, leaving an 18"/45.7cm tail. Using photo as a guide, sew on tail.

This project was made with 1 skein of
Caron's Simply Soft in (100% acrylic, 3.5oz/100g, 166yd/152 m), in #2705, Soft Green

June 31

Did I Just Say That?

The look on this mouse's face is just so cute and adoring. Maybe I'm twisted, but I think it would be funny to fill it with catnip and let your kitty tear it to shreds. Your cat will love it.

Werner the Wiener Dog

This amigurumi was inspired by a very cute illustration of a dachshund on a notebook I wrote my patterns in. I've always thought that it pays to surround yourself with images that you find appealing.

Skill Level
Intermediate

Finished Measurements
Approx 4"/10.2cm tall by 14"/35.6cm long

Materials
Worsted weight "soft-type" acrylic yarn:
  Color A: black
  Color B: coral
  Color C: light blue
  Color D: copper
See page 10 for tips on estimating yarn amounts.
Crochet hook:
  3.5mm/E-4 or size to obtain gauge
Polyester fiberfill
PVC pellets (optional)
Locking stitch marker
2 brown eyes, 15mm
Tapestry needle
Wool or wool-blend felt, red
Perle cotton, size 5, gold
Embroidery needle
Craft glue
11 silver seed beads, size 6
Small snap (for collar)
Template, page 127

Caution: The PVC pellets listed above are not child-safe. If you're making this project for a child, use polyester fiberfill for stuffing.

Gauge
5 rnd gauge circle = 2"/5cm
See page 32 for instructions on making a gauge circle.

Stitches and Techniques Used
Make ring (mr)
Single crochet (sc)
Invisible decrease (invdec), page 23
Changing colors, page 29
Half double crochet (hdc)
Back loop only (BLO)
Blanket stitch, page 30

Instructions

Head

Note: Head is worked in a continuous spiral. Do not join rnds. You may wish to use a marker to indicate the beginning of the rnd.

Starting at tip of nose, with 3.25mm/D-3 hook and color B, mr.

Rnd 1: Ch 1, 6 sc in first ch, pull starting ring closed (6 sc).

Rnd 2: 2 sc in each sc (12 sc).

Rnd 3: Inc 6 evenly (18 sc).

Rnd 4: Sc in each sc.

Rnd 5: Invdec 6 (12 sc).

Switch to color A before finishing last stitch, cut color B, and work over end. Stuff nose firmly after this rnd and while working rnd 6.

Rnd 6: Invdec 6 times (6 sc).

The tip of the nose should be a tight ball. Switch to 3.5mm/E-4 hook.

Rnds 7 and 8: Inc 3 evenly spaced (12 sc at end of rnd 8).

Note: Make sure to stuff the rest of nose as you go along.

Rnd 9: (Sc in next 3 sts, 2 sc in the next st) twice, hdc in the next 3 sts, 2 hdc in the next st (15 sts).

Rnd 10: Sc in the next 10 sts, hdc in the next 5 sts.

Rnd 11: (Sc in the next 4 sts, 2sc in the next st) twice, hdc in the next 4 sts, 2hdc in the next st (18 sts).

Rnd 12: Sc in the next 12 sts, hdc in the next 6 sts.

Rnd 13: (Sc in the next 5 sts, 2sc in the next st) twice, hdc in the next 5 sts, 2hdc in the next st (21 sts).

Rnd 14: (Sc in the next 6 sts, 2 sc in the next st) twice, hdc in the next 6 sts, 2 hdc in the next st (24 sts).

Rnd 15: (Sc in the next 3 sts, 2sc in the next st) 4 times, (hdc in the next 3 sts, 2hdc in the next st) twice (30 sts).

Rnd 16: (Sc in the next 4 sts, 2sc in the next st) 4 times, (hdc in the next 4 sts, 2hdc in the next st) twice (36 sts).

Rnd 17: Sc in the next 27 sts, hdc in the next 9 sts.

Rnd 18: Hdc in the next 3 st, sc in the next 27 st, hdc in the next 6 sts.

Rnd 19: Working in sc for the rest of the head, inc 3 sc evenly spaced (39 sc).

Rnd 20: Inc 3 sc evenly spaced (42 sc).

Rnd 21: Sc in each sc.

Stop here a second to put the eyes in. Put your working loop on a locking stitch marker to save it for later. The eyes go in the valley between rnds 17 and 18—three valleys in from the edge. Make sure the nose is stuffed firmly and curves up the happy way. Orient the nose so it's smack in the middle and the head kind of looks up at you. Play with the placement of the eyes until you're happy with the spacing. The farther apart the eyes, the more innocent the dog looks; the closer together, the more predatory—until they get so close that he looks cross-eyed. To place them as I've done in this piece, put the eyes 17 posts apart, which is very far apart and looks innocent and quite sad.

Replace working loop on hook and proceed to rnd 22.

Rnd 22: Invdec 6 evenly spaced (36 sc).

Rnds 23–26: Rep rnd 22 (12 sc at end of rnd 26).

Rnd 27: Invdec 3 evenly spaced (9 sc).

Finish stuffing head firmly.

Fasten off, leaving an 18"/45.7cm tail. Thread tail onto tapestry needle. Close hole as illustrated on page 26. Weave in end.

Body

Note: Body is worked in a continuous spiral. Do not join rnds. You may wish to use a marker to indicate the beginning of the rnd.

Starting at neck with 3.5mm/E-4 hook and color A, mr.

Rnd 1: Ch 1, 6 sc in ring, pull starting ring closed (6 sc).

Rnd 2: 2 sc in each sc (12 sc).

Rnd 3: Inc 6 evenly (18 sc).

Rnd 4: Working through BLO, sc in each sc.

Rnd 5: Working into both loops, sc in next 3 sc, sl st in next 6 sc, sc in next 3 sc, hdc in next 6 sc.

Rnd 6: (Sc in next 2 st, 2sc in next st) 6 times (24 sc).

Rnd 7: Sc in next 4 sc, sl st in next 8 sc, sc in next 4 sc, hdc in next 8 sc.

Rnd 8: (Sc in next 3 st, 2 sc in next st) 6 times (30 sc).

Rnd 9: Hdc in next 2 sc, sc in next 5 sc, sl st in next 10 sc, sc in next 5 sc, hdc in next 8 sc.

Note: When you come to the sl sts in the next rnd, work over them into the row below. This technique creates three-dimensional sculpting. Use this technique whenever sl sts are worked within the rnd for the remainder of this pattern.

Rnd 10: (Sc in next 4 st, 2 sc in next st) 6 times (36 sc).

Rnd 11: Hdc in next 4 sc, sc in next 6 sc, slst in next 12 sc, sc in next 6 st, hdc in next 8 sc.

Rnds 12–47: Sc in each sc.

Rnd 48-51: Invdec 6 sc evenly spaced (12 sc at end of rnd 51).

Rnd 52: Invdec 3 evenly spaced (9 sc).

Stuff body firmly.

Fasten off, leaving an 18"/45.7cm tail. Thread tail onto tapestry needle. Close hole as illustrated on page 26. Weave in end.

Right Legs (make 2)

Note: Legs are worked in a continuous spiral. Do not join rnds. You may wish to use a marker to indicate the beginning of the rnd.

Starting at bottom with 3.5mm/E-4 hook and color D, mr.

Rnd 1: Ch 1, 6 sc in ring, pull starting ring closed (6 sc).

Rnd 2: 2 sc in next st, (sc, hdc) in next st, 2 hdc in next st, (hdc, sc) in next st, 2 sc in next 2 sts (12 sts).

Rnd 3: 2 sc in next st, sc in next 2 sts, hdc next st, 3 hdc in next st, hdc in next st, 3 hdc in next st, hdc in next st, sc in next 2 sts, 2 sc in next 2 sts, sc in next st (18 sts).

Rnd 4: Sc in each st (18 sc).

Rnd 5: Sc in next 5 sc, invdec, sc in next 3 sc, invdec, sc in next 6 sc (16 sts).

Rnd 6: Sc in next 4 sts, invdec, sc in next 3 st, invdec, sc in next 5 sc (14 sts).

Change to color A.

Rnd 7: Sl st in next 8 sts, hdc in next 6 sts.

Rnds 8 and 9: Sc in next 8 sts, hdc in next 6 sts.

Rnd 10 (short rnd): Sc in next 2 sc. Do not finish rnd.

Stuff legs, preferably using PVC pellets as this will help the doggie to stand better. If you don't want to use the pellets for safety reasons, just stuff the legs a little extra firmly. Pinch each leg shut and make 6 sc across the top working through both thicknesses, making sure that the stuffing remains inside.

Fasten off, leaving an 18"/45.7cm tail. You will use this tail to whipstitch the legs onto the body later.

Left Legs (make 2)

Note: Legs are worked in a continuous spiral. Do not join rnds. You may wish to use a marker to indicate the beginning of the rnd.

Starting at bottom with 3.5mm/E-4 hook and color D, mr.

Work rnds 1–6 of Right Legs.

Rnd 7: Hdc in next 6 st, sl st in next 8 sts.

Rnds 8 and 9: Hdc in next 6 st, sc in next 8 sts.

Rnd 10 (short Rnd): Sc in next 2 sc.

Follow stuffing and fastening off instructions for Right Legs.

Ears (make 2)

Note: Ears are worked in a continuous spiral. Do not join rnds. You may wish to use a marker to indicate the beginning of the rnd.

Starting at bottom, with 3.5mm/E-4 hook and color D, mr.

Rnd 1: Ch 1, 6 sc in ring, pull starting ring closed (6 sc).

Rnd 2: 2 sc in each st (12 sc).

Rnds 3–7: Inc 6 sc evenly spaced (42 sc at the end of rnd 6).

Rnd 8: Invdec over next 2 sts, sc in next 17 sts, (invdec over next 2 sts) twice, sc in next 17 sts, invdec over next 2 sts (38 sts).

Fasten off, leaving an 24"/61cm tail. Fold ear in half with the decreases at the folds and use the yarn tail to whipstitch the ear closed. Do not weave in end; save it for whipstitching ear to head.

Tail (make 1)

The tail is made at a very tight gauge. Be sure to stuff as you go. You will never get the stuffing in afterward.

Note: Tail is worked in a continuous spiral. Do not join rnds. You may wish to use a marker to indicate the beginning of the rnd.

Starting at tip of tail, with 2.75mm/C-2 hook and color D, mr.

Rnd 1: 4 sc in ring, pull starting ring closed (4 sc).

Rnd 2: Inc 2 sc evenly spaced (6 sc).

Rnd 3: Inc 1 sc (7 sc).

Rnd 4: Sc in each sc.

Rnds 5–10: Rep last 2 rnds 3 times (10 sc at end of rnd 10).

Rnds 11–28: Sc in each sc.

Make certain that tail is stuffed very firmly. I stuff these so firmly that they are posable without the use of any armature.

Fasten off, leaving an 18"/45.7cm tail. You will use the yarn tail to whipstitch the dog's tail on to the body later.

Assembly

Using photo as a guide, whipstitch ears to head. The seam that you sewed shut when you folded the ear in half faces out.

Cut a 12"/30.5cm length of color D and whipstitch the head to the neck using the photo as a guide. The free front loop on rnd 4 of the body is very useful for sewing into and making sure that the head goes on straight.

Using the photo as a guide, pin the legs to the body, making sure that the dog is balanced. Whipstitch the legs to the body.

Tip: the legs should be very far apart from each other, almost at the rounded ends of the body.

Using the photo as a guide, pin the tail to the body, making sure it is centered. Whipstitch the tail to the body.

Heart Appliqué

Cut a heart from the felt, using the template on page 127 as a guide.

Work blanket stitch around the edge in Perle cotton using embroidery needle.

Glue the heart to the wiener dog's bum using straight pins to keep it in place while it dries.

Collar (make 1)

String the seed beads onto color C (see page 29) before you begin to crochet.

With 2.75mm/C-2 hook and color C, ch 25.

Row 1: Sc 2nd ch from hook and every ch until end, pulling up a bead in the 3rd sc and in every other sc

thereafter until you run out of beads.

Note: A tip from the perfectionist: The collar will look nicer and much more even if you work into the bump of the starting ch instead of the more conventional method of splitting the V.

Fasten off. Weave in ends. Sew on small snap so that the collar fits tightly around neck.

This project was made with 1 skein each of

Color A: Caron's Simply Soft (100% acrylic, 3.5oz/100g, 166yd/152m), in #2680, Black

Color B: Simply Soft Brites (100% acrylic, 3.5oz/100g, 166yd/152m), in #2603, Papaya

Color C: Bernat's Satin (100% acrylic, 3.5oz/100g, 166yd/152m), in #04742, Lagoon

Color D: Caron's Simply Soft (100% acrylic, 3.5oz/100g, 166yd/152m), in #2714, Copper Kettle

May 2

The "Eyes" Have It

They say the eyes are the windows to the soul. A few of my 'gurumis are all about the eyes.

The look on Wiener Dog's face epitomizes "puppy dog eyes." If you feel the need for a softie that will gaze up at you in fervent if somewhat lazy-eyed admiration, well, Piglet is the doll for you.

Piglet

This little piggy…
started life as a sort of
uninspiring prairie-dog
type thing; I don't know
what I was thinking.
But it had potential, so
I reworked the pattern
into this much improved
piglet. Why the spots?
I can't stand to use just
one color on a design.

Skill Level

Intermediate

Finished Measurements

Approx 5½"/14cm tall by 5"/12.7cm
   wide

You Will Need

Worsted weight "soft-type" acrylic
   yarn:
      Color A: apricot
      Color B: coral
      Color C: aqua
      Color D: copper
Perle cotton, size 5
      Color E: cream
See page 10 for tips on estimating
   yarn amounts.
Crochet hooks:
      3.5mm/E-4 or size to obtain gauge
      3.25mm/D-3
      2.75mm/C-2
      1.4mm/9 steel hook
Tapestry needle
Locking stitch marker
2 blue eyes, 15mm
Invisible thread
Sewing needle
Perle cotton, size 5, dark brown
Embroidery needle
Polyester fiberfill
Wool or wool-blend felt, pink
Craft glue
Straight pins
Blush and cotton swabs
Templates, page 127

Gauge

5 rnd gauge circle = 2"/5cm
See page 32 for instructions on
   making a gauge circle.

Stitches and Techniques Used

Make ring (mr), page 17
Chain (ch)
Half double crochet (hdc)
Slip stitch (sl st)
Single crochet (sc)
Double crochet (dc)
Back loop only (BLO)
Invisible decrease (invdec), page 23
French knots, page 30
Stem stitch,
   page 30
Repeat (rep)
Skip (sk)

Instructions

Round Eye Patches (make 2)

Note: Eye Patches are worked in joined rnds. Starting ch at beginning of rnds counts as a stitch.

Starting at center, with 1.4mm/9 steel hook and color E, mr.

Rnd 1: Ch 2, 13 hdc in ring, sl st to join (14 sts).

Do not pull the starting ring closed. Leave it large enough to put the shaft of the eye into later.

Rnd2: Ch 2, hdc in same sp, hdc in next st, sc in next 3 sts, hdc in next st, 2 hdc in next st, 2 dc in next 7 st, do not sl st to join (23 sts).

Fasten off leaving a 12"/30.5cm tail. Thread tail onto small tapestry or embroidery needle. Make invisible join (see page 26). Weave in end.

Body and Head (make 1)

Starting at snout, with 3.5mm/E-4 hook and color A, mr.

Rnd 1: Ch 1, 6 sc in ring, pull starting ring closed (6 sc).

Rnd 2: Ch 1, 2 sc in each st (12 sc).

Rnd 3: Inc 6 sc evenly spaced (18 sc).

Rnd 4: Work even BLO.

Rnd 5: Sc in the next 6 st, (invdec) 3 times, sc in the next 6 sts (15 sts).

Rnd 6: Sc in the next 6 sts, 2 sc in the next 3 sts, sc in the next 6 sts (18 sc).

Rnd 7: Inc 6 sc evenly spaced (24 sc).

Rnds 8–13: Inc 3 sc evenly spaced (42 sc at the end of rnd 13).

Rnd 14 and 15: Sc in each sc.

Rnd 16: Sc in the next 14 sts, invdec, sc in the next 6 sts, invdec, sc in the next 7 sts, invdec, sc in the next 9 sts (39 sts).

Rnd 17: Sc in each st.

Rnd 18: Sc in the next 14 sts, invdec, sc in the next 5 sts, invdec, sc in the next 5 sts, invdec, sc in the next 9 sts (36 sts).

Take a break here a minute to make the pig's face. Put your working loop on a locking stitch marker to save it for later. Put the eye patches on the shafts of the eyes. You can tighten up the starting ring on the patches at this point if they seem really loose. Put the eyes with the eye patches now on the shafts in the valley between rnds 12 and 13, eighteen posts apart. Make sure to center the up-turn of the nose between the eyes. Take note that in the photo the wider part of the eye patch is downward, giving the piggy a questioning, almost teary-eyed look. Sew the eye patch in place using invisible thread and sewing needle. Use dark brown Perle cotton to make two French knots for nostrils. Use stem stitch for mouth.

Replace working loop on hook and proceed to rnd 19.

Rnd 19: Sc in each sc.

Rnd 20: Invdec 6 evenly (30 sts).

Rnd 21: Inc 3 sc evenly spaced (33 sc).

Rnd 22: Sc in each sc.

Rnds 23–30: Rep last 2 rnds 4 times (45 sc at the end of rnd 30).

Rnds 31–33: Inc 3 sc evenly spaced (54 sts at the end of rnd 33).

Rnd 34 and 35: Sc in each sc.

Rnd 36–42: Invdec 6 spaced evenly (12 sts at the end of rnd 42).

Stuff body.

Fasten off, leaving an 18"/45.7cm tail. Close hole as illustrated on page 26. Weave in end.

Front Legs (make 2)

Note: Legs are worked in a continuous spiral. Do not join rnds. You may wish to use a marker to indicate the beginning of the rnd.

Starting at bottom, with 3.5mm/E-4 hook and color A, mr.

Rnd 1: Ch 1, 6 sc in ring, pull starting ring closed (6 sts).

Rnd 2: 2 sc in the first st, (sc, hdc) in next st, 2 hdc in next st, (hdc, sc) in next st, (2 sc next st) twice (12 sts).

Rnd 3: 2 sc in the next st, sc in the next 2 sts, hdc in the next st, 3 hdc in the next st, hdc in the next st, 3 hdc in the next st, hdc in the next st, sc in next 2 sts, 2 sc in the next st, sc in the next st (18 sts).

Rnd 4: Sc in each st.

Rnd 5: Sc in next 5 sts, invdec, sc in the next 3 sts, invdec, sc in the next 6 sts (16 sts).

Rnd 6: Sc in next 5 sts, invdec, sc in the next st, invdec, sc in the next 6 sts (14 sts).

Rnd 7: Sc in next 4 sts, invdec, sc in the next st, invdec, sc in the next 5 sts (12 sts).

Rnds 8–11: Sc in each sc.

Rnd 12: (Invdec, sc in the next 2 sts) 3 times (9 sts).

Fasten off, leaving an 18"/45.7cm tail. Stuff foot. Close hole as illustrated on page 26. Weave in end.

Cut an 18"/45.7cm length of color A for each leg. Using the photo as a guide, whipstitch legs in place.

Cut two front feet soles out of felt using the template on page 127 as a guide. Glue them to bottoms of front feet, using straight pins to keep them in place while they dry.

Back Feet (make 2 with A)

Note: Back feet are worked in joined, oval-shaped rnds. Ch 1 at beginning of rnds 1–4 counts as a stitch.

Do not mr to begin and do not sl st to join rnds except as noted. At rnd 5, you begin working in spirals.

Rnd 1: With 3.5mm/E-4 hook and color A, ch 5, 2 sc in second ch from hook, sc in next 2 ch, 3 hdc in last ch, turn and work along the other side of the chain, working into the unused loops, sc in next 2 ch, sl st to the top of the first sc to join (join all following rnds in this manner until rnd 5) (10 sts).

Rnd 2: Ch 1 (at the beginning of this and every rnd until rnd 5), sc in same space, sc in next 3 sts, (sc, 2 hdc) in the next st, 2 hdc in the next st, (2 hdc, sc) in the next st, sc in next 3 sts, sl st to the top of the first sc to join (16 sts).

Rnd 3: Ch 1, 2 sc in same space, sc in next 4 sts, (sc, 2 hdc) in the next st, hdc in next 4 sts, (2 hdc, sc) in the next st, sc in next 3 sts, 2 sc in the next st, sl st to the top of the first sc to join (22 sts).

Rnd 4: Ch 1, sc in same space, sc in next 6 sts, (sc, 2

hdc) in the next st, hdc in next 6 sts, (2 hdc, sc) in the next st, sc in next 6, sl st to the top of the first sc to join (26 sts).

Rnd 5: Do not ch 1. Sk the sp you slst-ed into. Sc into the next st. See how your work is slanting? It should look like that. You have just switched to working a spiral. Congrats! Sc in the next 5 sts, invdec, sc in the next 7 sts, invdec, sc the 7 sts (23 sts).

Continue working in spirals for remainder of foot.

Rnd 6: Invdec, sc in the next 5 sts, (invdec) twice, sc in the next st, (invdec) twice, sc in the next 5 sts, invdec (17 sts).

Rnd 7: Invdec, sc in the next 5 sts, invdec over the next 3 sts, sc in the next 5 sts, invdec (13 sts).

Fasten off leaving an 18"/45.7cm tail. Stuff foot very lightly. Pinch hole closed so that it makes a straight seam and whipstitch it shut with the yarn tail. Weave in end. This seam is now at the bottom of the foot. Cut an 18"/45.7cm length of color A for each foot. Using photo as a guide, whipstitch feet in place using yarn and tapestry needle.

Cut two back feet soles out of felt using the template on page 127 as a guide. Glue them to bottom of back feet using straight pins to keep them in place while they dry.

Ears (make 2)

Note: Ears are worked in a continuous spiral. Do not join rnds. You may wish to use a marker to indicate the beginning of the rnd.

Starting at tip, with 3.5mm/E-4 hook and color A, mr.

Rnd 1: Ch 1, 4 sc in ring, pull starting ring closed (4 sc).

Rnds 2–8: Inc 2 sc evenly spaced (18 sc at the end of rnd 8).

Rnds 9 and 10: Sc in each sc.

Fasten off leaving a 18"/45.7cm tail. Flatten ear and fold in half. There should be four layers of crochet. Using the yarn tail, whipstitch these layers together. Dab a bit of blush in the ears using the cotton swabs. Do not weave in end; instead, referring to photo as a guide, use it to whipstitch ears to head.

Tail (make 1)

With 2.75mm/C-2 hook and color A, ch 9 leaving an 18"/45.7cm tail at the beginning; turn.

Row 1: Sk the first ch, sc in the next 2 ch, 2 sc in the next 6 chs (14 sc).

Fasten off leaving a 18"/45.7cm tail. Using both yarn tails, sew the pig's tail to its body.

Spots

Note: Spots are worked in joined rnds. Chs at beginning of rnds count as a stitch.

Large (make 1 of each out of colors B, C, and D)

Starting at center, with 2.75mm/C-2 hook, mr.

Rnd 1: Ch 2, 7 hdc in ring, sl st to join, pull starting ring closed (8 sts).

Rnd 2: Ch 2, hdc in same space, 2 hdc in each st. Do not sl st (16 sts).

Fasten off leaving a 12"/30.5cm tail. Thread yarn onto tapestry needle. Make invisible join (see page 26 for instructions). Weave in end.

Small (make 1 of each out of colors B, C, and D)

Starting at center, with 2.75mm/C-2 hook, mr.

Rnd 1: Ch 1, 6 sc in ring, do not join, pull starting ring closed (7 sts).

Fasten off leaving a 12"/30.5cm tail. Thread yarn onto tapestry needle. Make invisible join (see page 26 for instructions). Weave in end.

Referring to the photo, sew the spots onto the pig's back and rump using the sewing needle and invisible thread.

This project was made with 1 skein each of

Color A: Caron's Simply Soft (100% acrylic, 3.5oz/100g, 166yd/152m), in #2715, Seashell

Color B: Caron's Simply Soft Brites (100% acrylic, 3.5oz/100g, 166yd/152m), in #2603, Papaya

Color C: Caron's Simply Soft Brites (100% acrylic, 3.5oz/100g, 166yd/152m), in #2608, Blue Mint

Color D: Caron's Simply Soft (100% acrylic, 3.5oz/100g, 166yd/152m), in #2714, Copper Kettle

Color E: DMC's Perle cotton, size 5, in #0002, Ecru

Friends Forever Fawn

Straight out of a children's fairytale, this sweet fawn's eyes will melt your heart.

Skill Level

Advanced

Finished Measurements

Approx 8"/20.3cm tall by 7"/17.8cm long

You Will Need

Worsted weight "soft-type" acrylic yarn:
   Color A: black
   Color B: copper
   Color C: pale gold
See page 10 for tips on estimating yarn amounts.
Crochet hooks:
   3.5mm/E-4 or size to obtain gauge
   2.75mm/C-2
Locking stitch marker
Wool or wool-blend felt, burgundy
Wool or wool-blend felt, pink
Perle cotton, size 5, black
Embroidery needle
2 black eyes, 15mm
Polyester fiberfill
Tapestry needle
Blush and cotton swabs
PVC pellets
Knee-high nylon (optional)
Invisible thread
Beading needle
Approx 13 flat white sequins
Approx 13 cream seed beads, size 10
Template, page 127

Caution: The PVC pellets listed above are not child-safe. This project is not appropriate for young children.

Gauge

5 rnd gauge circle = 2"/5cm
See page 32 for instructions on making a gauge circle.

Stitches and Techniques Used

Make ring (mr), page 17
Chain (ch)
Single crochet (sc)
Invisible decrease (invdec), page 23
Changing colors, page 29
Repeat (rep)
Back loop only (BLO)
Skip (sk)
Single crochet
   2 together
   (sc2tog)
Double crochet (dc)
Slip stitch (sl st)

Instructions

Head (make 1)

Note: Head is worked in a continuous spiral. Do not join rnds. You may wish to use a marker to indicate the beginning of the rnd.

Starting at front of muzzle, with color C and 3.5mm/E-4 hook, mr.

Rnd 1: Ch 1, 6 sc in ring, pull starting ring closed (6 sc).

Rnd 2: 2 sc in each st (12 sc).

Rnds 3 and 4: Inc 6 sc evenly spaced (24 sc at the end of rnd 4).

Rnd 5: Sc in next 8 sts, (invdec over next 2 sts, sc in next st) twice, invdec over next 2 st, sc in next 8 sts (21 sts).

Rnd 6: Sc in next 8 sts, (invdec over next 2 sts) 3 times, sc in next 7 sts (18 sts).

Switch to color B.

Rnd 7: Inc 6 sc evenly spaced (24 sc).

Rnd 8: Inc 3 sc evenly spaced (27 sc).

Rnd 9: Sc in each sc.

Rnds 10–19: Rep rnds 8 and 9 (42 st at the end of rnds 18 and 19).

Rnds 20–24: Invdec 6 sc evenly spaced (12 st at the end of rnd 24).

Put your working loop on a locking stitch marker to save it for later.

Cut eye patches out of felt using the template on page 127 as a guide. Glue the pink circles to the burgundy almond shapes and allow the glue to dry. With black perle cotton, using photo as a guide, embroider eyelashes, making sure to reverse the direction of the lashes for each eye.

Put the eyes with the eye patches on the shafts in the valley between rnds 13 and 14, sixteen posts apart. Make sure to center the up-turn of the muzzle between the eyes.

Fasten off, leaving an 18"/45.7cm tail.

Stuff head, making sure to stuff all the way into muzzle.

Thread yarn tail onto tapestry needle. Close hole as illustrated on page 26. Weave in end.

Nose (make 1)

Note: Nose is worked in a continuous spiral. Do not join rnds. You may wish to use a marker to indicate the beginning of the rnd.

Starting at tip, with 2.5mm/C-2 hook and color A, mr.

Rnd 1: Ch 1, 6 sc in ring, pull starting ring closed (6 sts).

Rnd 2: 2 sc in each st (12 sts).

Rnds 3 and 4: Work even in sc.

Rnd 5: Invdec 3 sc evenly spaced (9 sts).

Stuff nose firmly.

Fasten off, leaving an 18"/45.7cm tail. Thread onto tapestry needle. Close hole as illustrated on page 26. Do not weave in end. Whipstitch nose to muzzle using yarn tail.

Ears (make 2)

Starting at tip, with 3.5mm/E-4 hook and color B, mr.

Rnd 1: Ch 1, 4 sc in ring, pull starting ring closed (4 sts).

Rnds 2–8: Inc 2 sc evenly spaced (18 st at the end of rnd 8).

Rnds 9 and 10: Work even in sc.

Fasten off leaving a 18"/45.7cm tail. Flatten ear and fold in half. There should be four layers of crochet. Using yarn tail, whipstitch these layers together. Do not weave in end. Dab a bit of blush in the ears using the cotton swabs.

Using photo as a guide, whipstitch ears to head.

Body (make 1)

Starting at neck, with 3.5mm/E-4) hook and color B, mr.

Rnd 1: Ch 1, 6 sc in ring, pull starting ring closed (6 sc).

Rnd 2: 2 sc in each st (12 sc).

Rnd 3: Working thru BLO for entire rnd, sc in next 2 sts, sl st in next 4 sts, sc in next 2 sts, hdc in next 4 sts (12 sts).

Note: When you come to the sl sts in the next round, work over them into the row below. This technique creates three-dimensional sculpting. Use this technique whenever sl sts are worked within the rnd for the remainder of this pattern.

Rnd 4: (Sc in next 3 sts, 2 sc in next st) twice, hdc in next 3 sts, 2 hdc in next st (15 sts).

Rnd 5: Sc in next 3 sts, sl st in next 5 sts, sc in next 2 sts, hdc in next 5 sts (15 sts).

Rnd 6: (Sc in next 4 sts, 2 sc in next sts) twice, hdc in next 4 sts, 2 hdc in next st (18 sts).

Rnd 7: Sc in next 3 sts, sl st in next 6 sts, sc in next 3 sts, hdc in next 6 sts (18 sts).

Rnd 8: (Sc in next 5 sts, 2 sc in next st) twice, hdc in next 5 sts, 2 hdc in next st (21 sts).

Rnd 9: (Sc in next 6 sts, 2 sc in next st) twice, hdc in next 6 sts, 2 hdc in next st (24 sts).

Rnd 10: (Sc in next 3 sts, 2 sc in next st) 4 times, (hdc in next 3 sts, 2 hdc in next st) twice (30 sts).

Rnd 11: (Sc in next 4 sts, 2 sc in next st) 4 times, (hdc in next 4 sts, 2 hdc in next st) twice (36 sts).

Rnd 12: Sc in next 27 sts, hdc in next 9 sts.

Rnd 13: Hdc in next 3 sts, sc in next 27 sts, hdc in next 6 sts.

Rnd 14: Hdc in next 6 sts, sc in next 27

sts, hdc in next 3 sts.

Rnd 15: Hdc in next 9 sts, sc in next 27 sts.

Rnds 16–21: Sc in each sc.

Rnds 22–25: Invdec 6 sc evenly spaced (12 sc at the end of rnd 25).

Fasten off, leaving an 18"/45.7cm tail. Stuff the body, making especially certain that the neck is stuffed firmly. I find that it helps the fawn to balance nicely if I put half a knee-high nylon filled with PVC pellets in its belly in addition to polyester fiberfill. To do this, stuff the fawn about halfway and put an empty knee-high that has been cut in half in its belly. Open the knee-high up and put a few small handfuls of pellets in it; tie it with an overhand knot and then finish off the stuffing with some more fiberfill.

Note: It is essential to put PVC pellets in legs or else fawn will not stand up properly.

Thread yarn tail onto tapestry needle. Close hole as illustrated on page 26. Weave in end.

Front Legs (make 2)

Note: Legs are worked in a continuous spiral. Do not join rnds. You may wish to use a marker to indicate the beginning of the rnd.

Starting at bottom, with 3.5mm/E-4 hook and color A, mr.

Rnd 1: Ch 1, 6 sc in ring, pull starting ring closed (6 sc).

Rnd 2: 2 sc in next st, (sc, hdc) in next st, 2 hdc in next st, (hdc, sc) in next st, 2 sc in next 2 sts (12 sts).

Rnd 3: 2 sc in next st, sc in next 2 sts, hdc next st, 3 hdc in next st, hdc in next st, 3 hdc in next st, hdc in next st, sc in next 2 sts, 2 sc in next st, sc in next st (18 sts).

Rnd 4: Sc in each sc.

Rnd 5: Sc in next 5 sts, invdec over next 2 sts, sc in next 3 sts, invdec over next 2 sts, sc in next 6 sts (16 sts).

Switch to color B.

Rnd 6: Sc in next 4 sts, invdec over next 2 sts, sc in next 3 sts, invdec over next 2 sts, sc in next 5 sts (14 sts).

Rnds 7 and 8: Sc in each sc.

Rnd 9: Sc in next 2 sts, invdec over next 2 sts, sc in next 10 sts (13 sts).

Rnd 10 and 11: Sc in each sc.

Rnd 12: Sc in next 9 sts, invdec over next 2 sts, sc in next 2 sts (12 sts).

Rnd 13–20: Sc in each sc.

Rnd 21: Sc in next 2 sts, 2 sc in next st, sc in next 9 sts (13 sc).

Rnd 22: Sc in next 12 sts, 2 sc in next st (14 sc).

Rnd 23: Sc in next 6 sts, 2 sc in next st, sc in next 7 sts (15 sc).

Rnd 24: Sc in next 2 sts, 2 sc in next st, sc in next 12 sts (16 sc).

Rnd 25: Sc in next 4 sts, 2 sc in next st, sc in next 11 sts (17 sc).

Rnd 26: Sc in next 2 sts, hdc in next st, 2 hdc in next 2 sts, hdc in next st, sc in next 11 sts (19 sts).

Rnd 27: Sc in next 3 sts, (invdec over next 2 sts) 3 times, sc in next 10 sts (16 sts).

Stuff each leg with PVC pellets. If you find that the PVC is popping out if the crochet, you can line the inside of the legs with half of a knee-high nylon before stuffing them to keep the pellets from coming out. Be thrifty and use the second top half of the nylon, too. Just knot the cut end with an overhand knot before using it.

Note: It is essential to put PVC pellets in legs or else fawn will not stand up properly.

Close Top of Leg

The next few rows neatly close the top of the fawn's leg and give you a handy tab for sewing the leg onto the body.

Row 1: Sc in next 5 sts. Turn with no ch. Pinch leg shut.

Row 2: Sc in next 7 sts through both thicknesses. Because you did not ch, the turn will be tight. To make this easier, sk the last st of row 1. Turn with no ch.

Row 3: Sk first st, sc in next 4 sts, sc2tog.

Fasten off leaving a 18"/45.7cm tail. Do not weave in end. Using photo as a guide, whipstitch front legs to body.

Hind Legs

Rep rnds 1–12 of Front Legs—12 sts.

Rnd 13-17: Work even in sc.

Rnd 18: (2 hdc in next st) twice, sc in next 4 sts, sl st in next 2 sts, sc in next 4 sts (14 sts).

Rnds 19 and 20: Work even in sc.

Rnd 21: Sc in next 4 sts, 2 sc in next st, sc in next 9 sts (15 sts).

Rnd 22: Sc in next 14 sts, 2 sc in next st (16 sts).

Rnd 23: Sc in next 9 sts, (2 sc in next st) twice, sc in next 5 sts (18 sts).

Rnd 24: Sc in next 9 sts, (invdec over next 2 sts) twice, sc in next 5 sts (16 sts).

Rnds 25 and 26: Work even in sc.

Work remainder of Hind Legs as for Front Legs, skipping rnd 27.

Tail (make 1)

Starting at tip, with 3.5mm/E-4 hook and color B, mr.

Rnd 1: ch 1, 4 sc in ring, pull starting ring closed (4 sts).

Rnds 2–6: Inc 2 sc evenly spaced (14 sts at the end of rnd 6).

Rnd 7: Work even in sc.

Fasten off leaving a 18"/45.7cm tail.

If desired, cut 1yd/91.4cm of yarn in color D, unwind the strands, and use two of them to embroider straight stitches on the underside of the tail.

Flatten tail and fold in half. There should be four layers of crochet. Using yarn tail, whipstitch these layers together. Do not weave in end. Using photo as a guide, whipstitch tail to body.

Cut a 12"/30.5cm length of color B and whipstitch the head to neck using the photo as a guide. The free front loop on rnd 3 of the body is very useful for sewing into; note that unlike Werner the Weiner Dog, whose head was sewn on straight, the Fawn's head is at a slight angle.

Using photo as a guide, sew sequins and beads on to the fawn's back.

This project was made with 1 skein each of

Color A: Caron's Simply Soft (100% acrylic, 3.5oz/100g, 166yd/152m), in #2680, Black

Color B: Caron's Simply Soft (100% acrylic, 3.5oz/100g, 166yd/152m), in #2714, Copper Kettle

Color C: Caron's Simply Soft (100% acrylic, 3.5oz/100g, 166yd/152m), in #2713, Buttercup

May 20

The Feminine Mystique

Where did this fawn pattern come from? I don't know. I must have been getting in touch with my girly side; she's all feminine and fancy, and I'm not that way at all.

Humanoids

Ta-da…the final chapter! I must admit that these humanoid creatures who walk on their hind legs and wear people clothes are my special favorites. I think these softies appeal to me more because I feel like I can give them quite individual personalities.

When designing a new humanoid, I start by making the creature's head. I add facial features that occur to me as I go along—fangs, eyelashes, nostrils—you get the idea. It's during this process that I'm getting to know the personality of the amigurumi. That's why it doesn't take much longer to complete the rest of the doll, relatively speaking; by the time I'm done with their heads they've told me what they want to wear.

These dolls are all based on the same basic body pattern, with variations for different animals as well as what they are wearing. At the risk of sounding like a broken record, these patterns are in approximate order of difficulty. After making a few of them, I'm confident that you'll think of ways to make them your own. That's where the real fun comes in, when you start adding your unique touches. So get ready— you're about to learn the techniques you need to become a true amigurumi expert.

Hep Cat

In my family we are sort
of word dorks, so when it
occurred to me to make
a hep cat that was an
actual feline, well, that
was too good to pass up.
He's even got a soul patch!

Skill Level

Intermediate

Finished Measurements

Approx 13"/33cm tall

You Will Need

Worsted weight "soft-type" acrylic yarn:
- Color A: heather gray
- Color B: black
- Color C: cream
- Color D: aqua

Perle cotton, size 5
- Color E: light gray

See page 10 for tips on estimating yarn amounts.

Crochet hooks:
- 3.5mm/E-4 or size to obtain gauge
- 3mm/D-3
- 3.75mm/F-5
- 4mm/G-6
- 1.4mm/9 steel hook

2 eyes of any color, 9mm (for arm joints)
Tapestry needle
Perle cotton, size 5, black
Embroidery needle
2 blue cat eyes, 15mm
Invisible thread
Sewing needle
Locking stitch marker
Polyester fiberfill
PVC pellets (optional)

Knee-high nylon (if using PVC pellets)
Large-headed seaming pins

Caution: The PVC pellets listed above are not child-safe. If you're making this project for a child, use polyester fiberfill for stuffing.

Gauge

5 rnd gauge circle = 2"/5cm
See page 32 for instructions on making a gauge circle.

Stitches and Techniques Used

Make ring (mr), page 17
Chain (ch)
Single crochet (sc)
Invisible decrease (invdec), page 23
Bobble, page 22
Changing colors, page 29
Slip stitch (sl st)
Half double crochet (hdc)
Front loop only (FLO)

Instructions

Note: Sometimes, before or after a color change, I work an uncounted rnd of sl sts as indicated in the instructions. Do not work back into the sl sts. Instead, work the next rnd into the loops at the top of the rnd below. This smoothes out the color change. Be careful to keep your stitch count correct. If you find this difficult, you can skip these rows and work chain stitch embroidery to cover the color change after you are finished crocheting the doll. It gives the same effect but leaves more ends to weave in.

Arm (make 2)

Note: Arms are worked in a continuous spiral. Do not join rnds. You may wish to use a marker to indicate the beginning of the rnd.

Starting at fingertips, with 3.5mm/E-4 hook and color A, mr.

Rnd 1: Ch 1, work 6 sc in ring, pull starting ring closed (6 sc).

Rnd 2: 2 sc in each sc around (12 sc).

Rnd 3: *2 sc in next sc, sc in next sc; rep from * around (18 sc).

Rnds 4 and 5: Sc in each sc.

Rnd 6: Sc in next 16 sc, invdec over last 2 sc (17 sc).

Rnd 7: Sc in next 7 sts, invdec over next 2 sts, sc in next 7 sts, make bobble in next st (16 sts).

Switch to color B. Work an uncounted rnd of sl st.

Rnd 8: Sc in next 14 sts, invdec over next 2 sts (15 sts).

Rnd 9: Invdec over next 2 sts, sc in next 13 sts (14 sts).

Rnd 10: Sc in next 6 sts, invdec over next 2 sts, sc in next 6 sts (13 sts).

June 31

Hip Clothes for Hep Cat

It took me a while to decide what sort of pants a hipster like this guy would wear. I finally decided on powder blue, 1970s bell-bottom dress pants that are ubiquitous at thrift stores. Hep Cat doesn't have much money for clothes, of course. He writes poetry and spends what little he has on coffee.

Rnd 11: Sc in next 11 sts, invdec over next 2 sts (12 sts).

Rnd 12: Sc in next 4 sts, invdec over next 2 sts, sc in next 6 sts (11 sts).

Rnd 13: Sc in next 9 sts, invdec over next 2 sts (10 sts).

Rnds 14–33: Sc in each sc.

Fasten off, leaving an 18"/45.7cm tail. Stuff arm.

To make the shoulder joint, put a 9mm eye inside each arm with the shaft poking out in the first valley down from the top, lining up with the bobble thumb. Put a bit more stuffing on top of the shoulder. Close hole as illustrated on page 26. Weave in ends. Use an 18"/45.7cm length of yarn to sew through both layers of the arm to create a dent for the elbow in 12th valley down from top.

Muzzle (make 1)

Note: Muzzle is worked in a continuous spiral. Do not join rnds. You may wish to use a marker to indicate the beginning of the rnd.

Starting at bottom, with 3mm/D-3 hook and color C, mr.

Rnd 1: Ch 1, 6 sc in ring, pull starting ring closed (6 sc).

Rnd 2: Inc 6 sts (12 sc).

Rnds 3–8: Sc in each sc.

Rnd 9: (Invdec, sc in next 2 st) 3 times (9 sts).

Fasten off, leaving an 18"/45.7cm tail. Stuff muzzle lightly. Close hole as illustrated on page 26. Weave in end.

Using black Perle cotton and photo as a guide, embroider mouth on muzzle.

Cut a 24"/61cm length of color A. Using the photo as a guide, with two strands of color A and the embroidery needle, use satin stitch to embroider the soul patch. Set muzzle aside for later.

Ears (make 2)

Note: Ears are worked in a continuous spiral. Do not join rnds. You may wish to use a marker to indicate the beginning of the rnd.

Starting at tip, with 3mm/D-3 hook and color A, mr.

Rnd 1: Ch 1, 4 sc in ring, pull starting ring closed (4 sts).

Rnds 2–5: Inc 2 sc evenly spaced (12 sts at the end of rnd 5).

Fasten off, leaving an 18"/45.7cm tail. Do not weave in end. Set aside for later.

Pointed Eye Patches (make 2)

Starting at center of Eye Patch, with 1.4mm/9 steel hook and color E, mr.

Rnd 1: Ch 3 (counts as 1 dc), 13 dc in ring, join with sl st in top of beginning ch-3, do not pull starting ring closed (14 sts).

Do not pull the starting ring closed. Leave it large enough to put the shaft of the eye into later.

Rnd 2: Ch 2, hdc in same space as join, hdc in next st, sc in next st, (hdc, dc, hdc, in next st), sc in the next st, hdc in the next st, 2 hdc in next st, 2 dc in next 7 sts, do not join (24 sts).

Fasten off leaving a 12"/30.5cm tail. Make invisible join as illustrated on page 26. Weave in end.

Insert eye shaft into ring. Pull gently on tail of starting ring to snug around eye shaft. Set aside for later.

Body (make 1)

Note: Body is worked in a continuous spiral. Do not join rnds. You may wish to use a marker to indicate the beginning of the rnd.

Starting at top of head, with 3.5mm/E-4 hook and color A, mr.

Rnd 1: Ch 1, work 6 sc in ring, pull starting ring closed (6 sts).

Rnd 2: 2 sc in each sc around (12 sc).

Rnds 3–5: Inc 6 sc evenly spaced around. Avoid placing increases in the same place every round (30 sc at end of rnd 5).

Rnds 6–13: Inc 3 sc evenly spaced around (54 sc at end of rnd 13).

Rnds 14 and 15: Sc in each sc.

Rnds 16–19: Sc around, invdec 6 times evenly spaced around. Avoid placing decreases in the same place every round (30 sc at end of rnd 19).

Rnd 20: (Invdec over next 2 sts) 15 times (15 sc).

Place working yarn loop on a locking stitch marker and position the yarn tail at the back of the head. You'll now assemble the head.

The eyes go in place first. If you look at the texture of the crochet you'll see that the rounds form ridges and valleys. If you look even closer at the texture you'll see tiny posts in the valleys between rounds. Place the eyes on the posts in the third valley above the first decrease round. Another way of saying this is to put them between rounds 13 and 14, thirteen posts apart, making sure eyes are centered in the doll's face. Once you know where you want the eyes to be use something like the end of a rattail comb to poke a large hole into the crochet. Don't worry about hurting the crochet; it should be quite strong since you used such a small hook. Poke the eye shafts through to the inside of the head and fasten with the washers that came with them.

Stuff the head. Pin the muzzle and ears in place using large-headed seaming pins.

Referring to the photo for guidance, use invisible thread to sew the muzzle onto the head, placing it between the eyes. Using the yarn tails you left on the ears and a tapestry needle, sew them in place. Weave the ends in to the head.

Make sure the head is stuffed firmly. Now that the head is rounded out, tack the eye patches down with invisible thread as well. Replace working loop on hook and proceed to rnd 21.

Switch to color B.

Rnd 21: Inc 3 sc evenly spaced around (18 sc).

Rnd 22: Sc in each sc.

Rnds 23 and 24: Rep rnds 21 and 22 (21 sc at end of rnd 24).

To attach arms, put the eye shafts at the shoulders into body in the valley between rnds 22 and 23, eleven posts apart in the front. Put washers on eye shafts to secure arms.

Rnds 25–34: Rep last 2 rnds 5 times (36 sc).

Rnds 35–38: Sc in each sc around.

Work an uncounted rnd of sl sts.

Switch to color D.

Rnds 39–42: Sc in each sc around.

Stuff the body, using polyester fiberfill or PVC pellets.

Now the body will be divided to form the legs. Place the working yarn loop on a locking stitch marker. You should have a head with a tubular body and arms attached.

Find the center front point. This point lies along the lower edge of the body and lines up with the nose of your creature. Place a pin (large-headed seaming pins are particularly useful for this) or stitch marker between two stitches to mark the center front point. Count 18 stitches on either side of the center point. Place a second stitch marker or pin between two stitches at the center back. The center front and back points divide the body into a left half and a right half.

Left Leg and Pant

Pant: Put working loop back on hook. Begin working pant leg as follows.

Rnd 1: Sc in each sc to the center back marker, sk next 18 sts (leaving them for Right Leg), remove markers, sc in each sc to the end of the round (18 sts).

Rnds 2–4: Sc in each sc.

Rnd 5: Inc 1 sc (19 sc).

Rnd 6: Sc in each sc.

Rnds 7–10: Rep rnds 5 and 6 twice (21 sc at end of rnd 10).

Switch to 3.75mm/F-5 hook.

Rnd 11: Inc 1 sc (22 sc).

Rnd 12: Working thru FLO, sc in each sc.

Rnds 13–16: Rep rnds 5 and 6 twice (24 sc at end of rnd 16).

Rnds 17–22: Inc 1 sc (30 sc at end of rnd 28).

Switch to 4mm/G-6 hook.

Rnds 23–28: Inc 1 sc (36 sc at end of rnd 28).

Rnd 29: Sc in each sc.

Rnd 30: Sl st in each sc.

Fasten off, leaving an 18"/45.7cm tail. Weave in end.

Leg: Roll pant leg back to expose back loop of rnd 11. Pull up a loop of color A in last stitch of rnd 11 and begin working leg as follows.

Rnd 12: Working in the unused loop of rnd 11, sc in first st of rnd 11 and in next 21 st. Your last sc goes in the st you joined yarn in (22 sts).

Rnds 13–28: Work even.

Mark center front stitch of leg with pin or stitch marker.

Rnd 29: Sc in each sc to 2 sc before marker, 3 hdc in next sc, hdc in next sc, (next sc should be marked), remove marker and hdc in next sc, hdc in next sc, 3 hdc in next sc, sc in each sc to end of rnd (26 sts).

Rnd 30: Sc in each st until 2nd hdc of rnd 29, 3 hdc in next st, hdc in next 5 sts, 3 hdc in next st, sc in each st to end of rnd (30 sts).

Rnd 31: Sc in each sc until 2nd hdc of rnd 30, 3 hdc in next st, hdc in next 7 sts, 3 hdc in next st, sc in each st to end of rnd (34 sts).

Left Bobble Toes

Rnd 32: Work as follows. Note that the bobbles are made with a different number of sts to create toes that are different sizes.

Sc in each sc until 3rd hdc of rnd 31.

Make bobble in next st: (YO, insert hook in st, YO and draw up a loop, YO

and draw through 2 loops on hook) 6 times, YO and draw through all 7 loops on hook.

Sc in next st.

Make bobble in next st: (YO, insert hook in st, YO and draw up a loop, YO and draw through 2 loops on hook) 5 times, YO and draw through all 6 loops on hook.

Sc in next st.

Make bobble in next st: sc in next st, (YO, insert hook in st, YO and draw up a loop, YO and draw through 2 loops on hook) 4 times, YO and draw through all 5 loops on hook.

Sc in next st.

Make bobble in next st: (YO, insert hook in st, YO and draw up a loop, YO and draw through 2 loops on hook) 4 times, YO and draw through all 5 loops on hook.

Sc in next st.

Make bobble in next st: (YO, insert hook in st, YO and draw up a loop, YO and draw through 2 loops on hook) 3 times, YO and draw through all 4 loops on hook, sc in each st to end of rnd—34 sts.

Fasten off, leaving an 18"/45.7cm tail. Weave in end. Stuff the leg with polyester fiberfill.

Right Leg and Pant

With the 'gurumi's back facing you, sk 7 st; join color A in next sc.

Rnd 1: Sc in each sc around (18 sts).

Rnds 2–31: Work as for rnds 2–31 of Left Leg and Pant.

Right Bobble Toes

Rnd 32: Work as follows. Note that the bobbles are made with a different number of sts to create toes that are different sizes.

Sc in each sc until 3rd hdc of rnd 31.

Make bobble in next st: (YO, insert hook in st, YO and draw up a loop, YO and draw through 2 loops on hook) 3 times, YO and draw through 4 loops on hook.

Sc in next st.

Make bobble in next st: (YO, insert hook in st, YO and draw up a loop, YO and draw through 2 loops on hook) 4 times, YO and draw through 5 loops on hook.

Sc in next st.

Make bobble in next st: (YO, insert hook in st, YO and draw up a loop, YO and draw through 2 loops on hook) 4 times, YO and draw through 5 loops on hook.

Sc in next st.

Make bobble in next st: (YO, insert hook in st, YO and draw up a loop, YO and draw through 2 loops on hook) 5 times, YO and draw through 6 loops on hook.

Sc in next st.

Make bobble in next st: (YO, insert hook in st, YO and draw up a loop, YO and draw through 2 loops on hook) 6 times, YO and draw through 7 loops on hook, sc in each st to end of rnd (34 sts).

Fasten off, leaving an 18"/45.7cm tail. Weave in end. Stuff the leg, using polyester fiberfill.

Sole of Foot (make 2)

Note: Soles of feet are worked in joined, oval-shaped rnds. Ch 1 at beginning of rnds counts as a stitch.

With 3mm/D-3 hook and color A, ch 7.

Rnd 1: Working in back bumps of foundation ch, sc in second ch from hook, sc in next 4 ch, 3 hdc in last ch; working along opposite side of beginning ch, sc in next 5 ch; join with sl st in first sc (14 sts).

Rnd 2: Ch 1, 2 sc in same st as join, sc in next 4 sts, 3 hdc in next st, hdc in next st, 3 hdc in next st, sc in next 4 sts, 3 sc in last st, join with sl st in first sc (21 sts).

Rnd 3: Ch 1, 2 sc in same st as join, sc in next 6 sts, 3 hdc in next st, hdc in next 3 sts, 3 hdc in next st, sc in next 8 sts, join with sl st in first sc (26 sts).

Rnd 4: Ch 1, 2 sc in same st as join, sc in next st, 2 sc in next st, sc in next 6 st, 3 hdc in next st, hdc in next 5 sts, 3 hdc

Instructions

Note: Sometimes, before or after a color change, I work an uncounted rnd of sl sts as indicated in the instructions. Do not work back into the sl sts. Instead, work the next rnd into the loops at the top of the rnd below. This smoothes out the color change. Be careful to keep your stitch count correct. If you find this difficult, you can skip these rows and work chain stitch embroidery to cover the color change after you are finished crocheting the doll. It gives the same effect but leaves more ends to weave in.

Arm (make 2)

Note: Arms are worked in a continuous spiral. Do not join rnds. You may wish to use a marker to indicate the beginning of the rnd.

Starting at fingertips, with 3.5mm/E-4 hook and color B, mr.

Rnd 1: Ch 1, work 6 sc in ring, pull starting ring closed (6 sc).

Rnd 2: 2 sc in each sc around (12 sc).

Rnd 3: *2 sc in next sc, sc in next sc; rep from * around (18 sc).

Rnds 4 and 5: Sc in each sc.

Rnd 6: Sc in next 16 sc, invdec over last 2 sc (17 sc).

Rnd 7: Sc in next 7 sts, invdec over next 2 sts, sc in next 7 sts, make bobble in next st (16 sts).

Rnd 8: Sc in next 14 sts, invdec over next 2 sts (15 sts).

Rnd 9: Invdec over next 2 sts, sc in next 13 sts (14 sts).

Change to color A.

Rnd 10: Sc in next 6 sts, invdec over next 2 sts, sc in next 6 sts (13 sts).

Dec 10

Barrelful of Monkeys

Benny the Monkey is one of my first Humanoid designs. I made a blue head on a whim and then was totally stuck. My mom decided it should be a monkey and helped pick out the rest of the colors, so she got to name him for the book.

Rnd 11: Sc in next 11 sts, invdec over next 2 sts (12 sts).

Rnd 12: Sc in next 4 sts, invdec over next 2 sts, sc in next 6 sts (11 sts).

Rnd 13: Sc in next 9 sts, invdec over next 2 sts (10 sts).

Rnds 14–28: Sc in each sc.

Switch to color C. Work an uncounted rnd of sl st.

Rnds 29–33: Sc in each sc.

Fasten off, leaving an 18"/45.7cm tail. Stuff arm. To make the shoulder joint, put a 9mm eye inside each arm with the shaft poking out in the first valley down from the top, lining up with the bobble thumb. Put a bit more stuffing on top of the shoulder. Close hole as illustrated on page 26. Weave in ends. Use an 18"/45.7cm length of yarn to sew through both layers of the arm to create a dent for the elbow in the 12th valley down from the top.

Face (make 1)

With 4.25mm/G-6 hook and color B, ch 14. Change to 3.5mm/E-4 hook.

Rnd 1: Working in back bumps of foundation ch, sc in second and each ch across (13 sc).

Rnd 2: Pivot work to work along opposite side of foundation, sk first sc, 6 dc in next sc, sk 1 sc, sc in next 7 sc, sk 1 sc, 6 dc in next sc, sk last sc; join with sl st to top of first sc in rnd 1 to join (32 st).

Rnd 3: Ch 2, (hdc, sc) in same st as join, sc in next 11 sc, (sc, hdc) in next sc, 2 dc in next 6 dc, hdc in next st, sk 2 sc, sl st in next sc, sk 2 sc, hdc in next st, 2 dc in next 6 dc, do not join.

Fasten off. Make an invisible join as illustrated on page 26. Weave in ends.

Put 12mm black eyes into stitches with 6 dcs in them. If the holes are not big enough, make them larger with the end of a rattail comb or something else pointy. Set face aside for later.

Muzzle (make 1)

Note: Muzzle is worked in a continuous spiral. Do not join rnds. You may wish to use a marker to indicate the beginning of the rnd.

Starting at bottom, with 3.5mm/E-4 hook and color B, mr.

Rnd 1: Ch 1, 6 sc in ring, pull starting ring closed (6 sc).

Rnd 2: Inc 6 sts (12 sc).

Rnds 3–23: Sc in each sc.

Rnd 9: (Invdec, sc in next 2 st) 3 times (9 sc).

Fasten off, leaving an 18"/45.7cm tail. Close hole as illustrated on page 26. Weave in end. Set muzzle aside for later.

Ears (make 2)

Note: Ears are worked in a continuous spiral. Do not join rnds. You may wish to use a marker to indicate the beginning of the rnd.

Starting at tip, with 3.5mm/E-4 hook and color A, mr.

Rnd 1: Ch 1, work 6 sc in ring; do not join, pull starting ring closed (6 sc).

Rnd 2: 2 sc in each sc around (12 sc).

Rnd 3: (Sc in next sc, 2 sc in next sc) 6 times (18 sc).

Rnd 4: (Sc in next 7 sc, invdec over next 2 sts) twice (16 sts).

Rnd 5: (Sc in next 6 sc, invdec over next 2 sts) twice (14 sts).

Rnd 6: (Sc in next 5 sc, invdec over next 2 sts) twice (12 sts).

Rnd 7: (Sc in next 4 sc, invdec over next 2 sts) twice (10 sts).

Fasten off, leaving an 18"/45.7cm tail for sewing ear to head. Set ear aside for later.

Body (make 1)

Note: Body is worked in a continuous spiral. Do not join rnds. You may wish to use a marker to indicate the beginning of the rnd.

Starting at top of head, with 3.5mm/E-4 hook and color A, mr.

Rnd 1: Ch 1, work 6 sc in ring, pull starting ring closed (6 sc).

Rnd 2: 2 sc in each sc around (12 sc).

Rnds 3–5: Inc 6 sc evenly spaced around. Avoid placing increases in the same place every round (30 sc at end of rnd 5).

Rnds 6–13: Inc 3 sc evenly spaced around (54 sc at end of rnd 13).

Rnds 14 and 15: Sc in each sc.

Rnds 16–19: Sc around, invdec 6 times evenly spaced around. Avoid placing decreases in the same place every round (30 sts at end of rnd 19).

Rnd 20: (Invdec over next 2 sts) 15 times (15 sts).

Place working yarn loop on a locking stitch marker and position the yarn tail at the back of the head. You'll now assemble the head.

The face and eyes are sewn on first. If you look at the texture of the crochet you'll see that the rounds form ridges and valleys. If you look even closer at the texture you'll see tiny posts in the valleys between rounds. Place the eyes (which are now connected to the face, of course) on the posts in the third valley above the first decrease round. Another way of saying this is to put them between rounds 13 and 14, thirteen posts apart, making sure eyes are centered in the doll's face. Once you know where you want the eyes to be, use something like the end of a rattail comb to poke a large hole into the crochet. Don't worry about hurting the crochet; it should be quite strong since you used such a small hook. Poke the eyes with the patches on the shafts through to the inside of the head and fasten with the washers that came with them. You may have to stretch the face a bit to get them to fit. That's OK.

Sew muzzle onto head in between eyes using invisible thread, using photo as a guide. Make a French knot with two strands of embroidery floss, or sew on one black size-8 seed bead for each nostril. With two strands of embroidery floss, embroider a straight line for the mouth using stem stitch.

Using the yarn tails you left on the ears and a tapestry needle, sew them in place. Weave the ends into the head.

For both the ears and the muzzle, it's helpful to stuff the head first, pin these things in place using large-headed pins, and then sew them on.

Make sure the head is stuffed firmly. After the head is rounded out, tack the face down with invisible thread as well.

Replace working loop on hook and switch to color C.

Work an uncounted rnd of sl sts.

Rnd 21: Sc around increasing 3 sc evenly spaced around (18 sc).

Rnd 22: Sc in each sc.

Rnds 23 and 24: Rep rnds 21 and 22 (21 sc).

To attach the arms, put the eye shafts at the shoulders into body in the valley between rnds 22 and 23, eleven posts apart in the front. Put washers on eye shafts to secure arms.

Rnds 25–34: Rep last 2 rnds 5 times (36 sc).

Rnds 35–37: Sc in each sc.

Work an uncounted rnd of sl sts.

Shorts

Switch to color D and 3.75mm/F-5 hook.

Rnd 1: Working through front loop only of st for entire rnd, sc in each sc around. When you get to the stitch just before the center back ch 3, sk 3 stitches. This is hole for the tail.

Rnd 2: Sc in each sc around, sc into the chs when you come to them (36 sc).

Rnds 3–8: Sc in each sc.

Rnd 9: Sl st in each sc.

Fasten off. Weave in ends.

Roll shorts to expose back loop of rnd 37. Pull up a loop of color A in the last stitch of rnd 37 and proceed as follows:

Rnds 38–42: Working into the unused loops of rnd 37 of body, sc in each sc.

Stuff the body, using polyester fiberfill or PVC pellets (if desired).

Now the body will be divided to form the legs. Place working yarn loop on a locking stitch marker or safety pin. You should have a head with a tubular body and arms attached.

Find center front point: This point lies along the lower edge of the body and lines up with the nose of your creature. Place a pin (large-headed seaming pins are particularly useful for this) or stitch marker between two stitches to mark center front point. Count 18 stitches on either side of the center point. Place a second stitch marker or pin between two stitches at the center back. The center front and back points divide the body into a left half and a right half.

Left Leg

Put working loop back on hook.

Rnd 1: Sc in each sc to the center back marker, sk next 18 sts (leaving them for Right Leg), remove markers, sc in each sc to the end of the round (18 sts).

Rnds 2–20: Sc in each sc.

Rnd 21: Sc in each sc around, inc once (19 sc).

Rnd 22: Sc in each sc.

Rnds 23–28: Rep last 2 rnds 3 times (22 sc).

Mark center front stitch of leg with pin or stitch marker.

Rnd 29: Sc in each sc to 2 sc before marker, 3 hdc in next sc, hdc in next sc, (next sc should be marked), remove marker and hdc in next sc, hdc in next sc, 3 hdc in next sc, sc in each sc to end of rnd (26 sts).

Switch to color B.

Rnd 30: Sc in each st until 2nd hdc of rnd 29, 3 hdc in next st, hdc in next 5 sts, 3 hdc in next st, sc in each st to end of rnd (30 sts).

Rnd 31: Sc in each sc until 2nd hdc of rnd 30, 3 hdc in next st, hdc in next 7 sts, 3 hdc in next st, sc in each st to end of rnd (34 sts).

Left Bobble Toes

Rnd 32: Work as follows. Note that the bobbles are made with a different number of sts to create toes that are different sizes.

Sc in each sc until 3rd hdc of rnd 31.

Make bobble in next st: (YO, insert hook in next st, YO and draw up a loop, YO and draw through 2 loops on hook) 6 times, YO and draw through all 7 loops on hook.

Sc in next st.

Make bobble in next st: (YO, insert hook in st, YO and draw up a loop, YO and draw through 2 loops on hook) 5 times, YO and draw through all 6 loops on hook.

Sc in next st.

Make bobble in next st:sc in next st, (YO, insert hook in st, YO and draw up a loop, YO and draw through 2 loops on hook) 4 times, YO and draw through all 5 loops on hook.

Sc in next st.

Make bobble in next st: (YO, insert hook in st, YO and draw up a loop, YO and draw through 2 loops on hook) 4 times, YO and draw through all 5 loops on hook.

Sc in next st.

Make bobble in next st: (YO, insert hook in st, YO and draw up a loop, YO and draw through 2 loops on hook) 3 times, YO and draw through all 4 loops on hook, sc in each st to end of rnd (34 sts).

Switch to color E.

Rnd 33: Sl st in each sc.

Fasten off, leaving an 18"/45.7cm tail. Weave in end. Stuff the leg with polyester fiberfill.

Right Leg

With the 'gurumi's back facing you, sk 7 st, Join color A in next sc.

Rnd 1: Sc in each sc around (18 sts).

Rnds 2–31: Work as for rnds 2–31 of Left Leg.

Right Bobble Toes

Rnd 32: Work as follows. Note that the bobbles are made with a different number of sts to create toes that are different sizes.

Sc in each sc until 3rd hdc of rnd 31.

Make bobble in next st: (YO, insert hook in st, YO and draw up a loop, YO and draw through 2 loops on hook) 3 times, YO and draw through 4 loops on hook.

Sc in next st.

Make bobble in next st: (YO, insert hook in st, YO and draw up a loop, YO and draw through 2 loops on hook) 4 times, YO and draw through 5 loops on hook.

Sc in next st.

Make bobble in next st: (YO, insert hook in st, YO and draw up a loop, YO and draw through 2 loops on hook) 4 times, YO and draw through 5 loops on hook.

Sc in next st.

Make bobble in next st: (YO, insert hook in st, YO and draw up a loop, YO and draw through 2 loops on hook) 5 times, YO and draw through 6 loops on hook.

Sc in next st.

Make bobble in next st: (YO, insert hook in st, YO and draw up a loop, YO and draw through 2 loops on hook) 6 times, YO and draw through 7 loops on hook, sc in each st to end of rnd (34 sts).

Switch to color E.

Rnd 33: Sl st in each sc.

Fasten off, leaving an 18"/45.5cm tail. Weave in end. Stuff the leg, using polyester fiberfill.

Sole of Foot (make 2)

Note: Soles of feet are worked in joined, oval-shaped rnds. Ch 1 at beginning of rnds counts as a stitch.

With 3mm/D-3 hook and color E, ch 7.

Rnd 1: Working in back bumps of foundation ch, sc in second ch from hook, sc in next 4 ch, 3 hdc in last ch; working along opposite side of beginning ch, sc in next 5 ch; join with sl st in first sc (14 sts).

Rnd 2: Ch 1, 2 sc in same st as join, sc in next 4 sts, 3 hdc in next st, hdc in next st, 3 hdc in next st, sc in next 4 sts, 3 sc in last st, join with sl st in first sc (21 sts).

Rnd 3: Ch 1, 2 sc in same st as join, sc in next 6 sts, 3 hdc in next st, hdc in next 3 sts, 3 hdc in next st, sc in next 8 sts, join with sl st in first sc (26 sts).

Rnd 4: Ch 1, 2 sc in same st as join, sc in next st, 2 sc in next st, sc in next 6 st, 3 hdc in next st, hdc in next 5 sts, 3 hdc in next st, sc in next 6 sts, 2 sc in next st, sc in next st, 2 sc in next st, do not join (34 sts).

Fasten off, leaving a 36"/91.4cm tail. Make invisible join as illustrated on page 26. Do not weave in end. Instead use it to whipstitch one sole onto each leg, making sure to line up corners of 3 hdcs. Whipstitch the sole of the foot into rnd 32 of the leg, leaving the entire sl st exposed. Stuff the foot, making sure as you do this that there is enough stuffing in the leg and that the corners at the front of the feet are filled out.

To make knees, sew a dent back and forth across the front of each leg with a short length of color A, stitching between rnds 10 and 11, five posts apart. Tie in a tight knot, and weave in ends.

Cut two 18"/45.7cm lengths of color E, and, using photo as a guide, use satin stitch to embroider lines for flip-flop thongs. Weave in ends.

Tail (make 1)

Note: Tail is worked in a continuous spiral. Do not join rnds. You may wish to use a marker to indicate the beginning of the rnd.

Stuff the tail with fiberfill as you crochet. Working the stuffing down to the very tip can be tricky.

Starting at tip, with 3.25mm/D-3 hook and color A, mr.

Rnd 1: Ch 1, work 6 sc in ring; do not join, pull starting ring closed (6 sc).

Rnd 2: 2 sc in each sc around (12 sc).

Rnd 3: Sc around, invdec once (11 sts).

Rnds 4–7: Sc in each sc.

Rnds 8–22: Rep rnds 3–7 three times; avoid placing decreases in the same place on each rnd (8 sts at end of rnd 19).

Rnds 23–32: Sc in each sc around.

Fasten off, leaving an 18"/45.7cm yarn tail for sewing the monkey's tail to the body. Stuff the tail with fiberfill. Pin tail to body through the hole in the shorts and sew in place. Weave in ends.

Pinch the shorts together between the legs. Sew closed with a short length of color D.

Star Appliqué

Cut a star out of felt using the template on page 127 as a guide.

Embroider blanket stitch around the edge using the Perle cotton and embroidery needle. Glue the star to the monkey's T-shirt, using straight pins to keep it in place while it dries.

This project was made with 1 skein each of

Color A: Caron's Simply Soft Brites (100% acrylic, 3.5oz/100g, 166yd/152m), in #2609, Berry Blue

Color B: Caron's Simply Soft Brites (100% acrylic, 3.5oz/100g, 166yd/152m), in #2607, Limelight

Color C: Red Heart's Soft (100% acrylic, 5oz/140g, approx 256yd/234m), in #5142, Cherry Red

Color D: Caron's Simply Soft (100% acrylic, 3.5oz/100g, 166 yd/152 m), in #2713, Buttercup

Color E: Caron's Simply Soft (100% acrylic, 3.5oz/100g, 166 yd/152 m), in #2680, Black

Punk Bunny

I have to admit I thought I was pretty clever when it occurred to me to make a two-colored pom-pom for this bunny's tail. It doesn't take much to amuse me, I guess.

Skill Level
Advanced

Finished Measurements
Approx 15"/38.1cm tall

You Will Need
Worsted weight "soft-type" acrylic yarn:
  Color A: black
  Color B: coral
  Color C: pale peach
  Color D: cream
  Color E: copper
  Color F: minty blue
  Color G: light aqua
Perle cotton size 5
  Color H: light green
See page 10 for tips on estimating yarn amounts.
Crochet hooks:
  3.5mm/E-4 or size to obtain gauge
  3mm/D-3
  3.75mm/F-5
  4mm/G-6
  1.4mm/9 steel hook
Tapestry needle
Polyester fiberfill
2 eyes of any color, 9mm (for arm joints)
2 black eyes, 12mm
Locking stitch markers
Invisible thread
Embroidery needle
Black embroidery floss
Pink perle cotton or embroidery floss

Large-headed seaming pins
PVC pellets (optional)
Knee-high nylon (if using PVC pellets)
2"/5.1cm pom-pom maker
Wool or wool-blend felt, white
2 flat black sequins
2 red seed beads
Craft glue
Straight pins
Template, page 127

Caution: The PVC pellets listed above are not child-safe. If you're making this project for a child, use polyester fiberfill for stuffing.

Gauge
5 rnd gauge circle = 2"/5cm
See page 32 for instructions on making a gauge circle.

Stitches and Techniques Used
Make ring (mr), page 17
Chain (ch)
Single crochet (sc)
Invisible decrease (invdec), page 23
Bobble, page 22
Changing colors, page 29
Slip stitch (sl st)
Double crochet (dc)
Half double crochet (hdc)
Front loop only (FLO)
Satin stitch, page 30
Stem stitch, page 30

April 1

Defense Mechanism

Don't let the skull on this little guy's shirt fool you. Really he's kind of timid and twitchy, like most rabbits. He wears this shirt hoping that people will leave him alone. If you were the new kid at the skateboard park, you might wear a shirt like this, too.

Instructions

Note: Sometimes, before or after a color change, I work an uncounted rnd of sl sts as indicated in the instructions. Do not work back into the sl sts. Instead, work the next rnd into the loops at the top of the rnd below. This smoothes out the color change. Be careful to keep your stitch count correct. If you find this difficult, you can skip these rows and work chain stitch embroidery to cover the color change after you are finished crocheting the doll. It gives the same effect but leaves more ends to weave in.

Arm (make 2)

Note: Arms are worked in a continuous spiral. Do not join rnds. You may wish to use a marker to indicate the beginning of the rnd.

Starting at fingertips, with 3.5mm/E-4 hook and color A, mr.

Rnd 1: Ch 1, work 6 sc in ring, pull starting ring closed (6 sc).

Rnd 2: 2 sc in each sc around (12 sc).

Rnd 3: *2 sc in next sc, sc in next sc; rep from * around (18 sc).

Rnds 4 and 5: Sc in each sc.

Rnd 6: Sc in next 16 sc, invdec over last 2 sc (17 sts).

Rnd 7: Sc in next 7 sts, invdec over next 2 sts, sc in next 7 sts, make bobble in next st (16 sts).

Rnd 8: Sc in next 14 sts, invdec over next 2 sts (15 sts).

Rnd 9: Invdec over next 2 sts, sc in next 13 sts (14 sts).

Change to color B. Work and uncounted rnd of sl st.

Rnd 10: Sc in next 6 sts, invdec over next 2 sts, sc in next 6 sts (13 sts).

Change to color C.

Rnd 11: Sc in next 11 sts, invdec over next 2 sts (12 sts).

Change back and forth between colors B and C every rnd for stripe pattern.

Rnd 12: Sc in next 4 sts, invdec over next 2 sts, sc in next 6 sts (11 sts).

Rnd 13: Sc in next 9 sts, invdec over next 2 sts (10 sts).

Rnds 14–33: Sc in each sc around, continuing to change colors for stripe pattern.

Fasten off, leaving an 18"/45.7cm tail. Stuff arm.

To make the shoulder joint, put a 9mm eye inside each arm with the shaft poking out in the first valley down from the top, lining up with the bobble thumb. Put a bit more stuffing on top of the shoulder. Close hole as illustrated on page 26. Weave in ends. Use an 18"/45.7cm length of yarn to sew through both layers of the arm to create a dent for the elbow in the 12th valley down from the top.

Muzzle (make 1)

Note: Muzzle is worked in joined rnds. Starting ch at beginning of rnds counts as a stitch.

Starting at bottom, with 3mm/D-3 hook and color D, mr.

Rnd 1: Ch 3, 11 dc in ring sl st to top of starting ch 3 to join (12 sts).

Rnd 2: Ch 2, hdc in same space as join, sc in next st, (hdc, dc, hdc) in next st, sc in next st, 2 hdc in next st, 2 dc in next 7 sts, do not join (23 sts).

Fasten off leaving a 18"/45.7cm tail. Make invisible join as illustrated on page 26. Weave in end.

Eye Patches (make 2)

Note: Eye Patches are worked in joined rnds. Starting ch at beginning of rnds counts as a stitch.

Starting at center of Eye Patch, with 1.4mm/9 steel hook and color H, mr. Leave starting ring large so eye can be inserted.

Rnd 1: Ch 3 (counts as 1 dc), 13 dc in ring, join with sl st in top of beginning ch-3, do not pull starting ring closed (14 sts).

Rnd 2: Ch 2, hdc in same space as join, hdc in next st, sc in next 3 st, hdc in the next st, 2 hdc in next st, 2 dc in next 7 sts, do not join (24 sts).

Fasten off, leaving a 12"/30.5cm tail. Make invisible join as illustrated on page 26. Weave in end. Insert eye shaft into ring. Pull gently on tail of starting ring to snug around eye shaft. Set aside for later.

Ears (make 2)

Note: Ears are worked in a continuous spiral. Do not join rnds. You may wish to use a marker to indicate the beginning of the rnd.

Starting at tip, with 3.5mm/E-4 hook and color A, mr.

Rnd 1: Ch 1, work 6 sc in ring (6 sc).

Rnd 2: 2 sc in each sc around (12 sc).

Rnd 3: Sc around increasing 6 sc evenly spaced around (18 sc).

Rnds 4–8: Sc in each sc.

Rnd 9: Sc in each sc around, invdec once (17 sc).

Rnd 10: Sc in each sc.

Rnds 11–20: Rep last 2 rnds 5 times; avoid placing decreases in the same place every round (12 sc at end of rnd 20).

Rnds 21–22: Sc in each sc.

Fasten off, leaving an 18"/45.7cm tail for sewing the ear to the body. Flatten ear and fold in half. There should be four layers of crochet. Use yarn tail to whipstitch these layers together. Leave remaining length of yarn to sew tail to body. Set aside for later.

Body (make 1)

Note: Body is worked in a continuous spiral. Do not join rnds. You may wish to use a marker to indicate the beginning of the rnd.

Starting at top of head, with 3.5mm/E-4 hook and color A, mr.

Rnd 1: Ch 1, work 6 sc in ring, pull starting ring closed (6 sc).

Rnd 2: 2 sc in each sc around (12 sc).

Rnds 3–5: Inc 6 sc evenly spaced around. Avoid placing increases in the same place every round (30 sc at end of rnd 5).

Rnds 6–13: Inc 3 sc evenly spaced around (54 sc at end of rnd 13).

Rnds 14 and 15: Sc in each sc.

Rnds 16–19: Sc around, invdec 6 times evenly spaced around. Avoid placing decreases in the same place every round (30 sts at end of rnd 19).

Rnd 20: (Invdec over next 2 sts) 15 times (15 sts).

Place working yarn loop on a locking stitch marked or safety pin and position the yarn tail at the back of the head. You'll now assemble the head.

The eyes go in place first. If you look at the texture of the crochet you will see that the rounds form ridges and valleys. If you look even closer at the texture you will see tiny posts in the valleys between rounds. Place the eyes with the patches on the posts in the third valley above the first decrease round. Another way of saying this is between rounds 13 and 14, thirteen posts apart, making sure the space in between them is centered in the front. Once you know where you want the eyes to be, use something like the end of a rattail comb to poke a large hole into the crochet. Don't worry about hurting the crochet; it should be quite strong since you used such a small hook. Poke the eyes through to the inside of the head and fasten with the washers that came with them.

Sew muzzle onto the head in between the eyes using invisible thread, referring to the photo for guidance. Once the muzzle is almost completely sewn in place, stuff a little bit behind it. After the muzzle is stuffed, embroider black lines for mouth and nose using 2 strands of floss. Use satin stitch to embroider the nose with 2 strands of pink embroidery floss or 1 length of perle cotton.

Using the yarn tails you left on the ears and a tapestry needle, sew them in place. Weave the ends in to the head.

For both the ears and the muzzle it's helpful to stuff the head first, pinning these things in place using large-headed pins, and then sewing them on. To embroider the muzzle after the head is stuffed, simply make a rather large knot on the end of your thread, pull it through a large hole in the crochet, and bring it up at a spot of denser texture in the muzzle. To finish, make a few very short stitches and pull them tight. They should become hidden in the texture of the crochet.

Make sure the head is stuffed firmly. After the head is rounded out, tack the eye patches down with invisible thread.

Replace working loop on hook and change to color B.

Work an uncounted rnd of sl sts.

Switch to color C.

Rnd 21: Inc 3 sc evenly spaced around (18 sc).

Rnd 22: Sc in each st around.

Rnds 23 and 24: Rep rnds 21 and 22 (21 sc at end of rnd 24).

To attach Arms, put the eye shafts at the shoulders into body in the valley between rnds 22 and 23, eleven posts apart in the front. Put washers on eye shafts to secure arms.

Rnds 25–34: Rep last 2 rnds 5 times (36 sc).

Rnds 35–38: Sc in each sc around.

Work an uncounted rnd of sl sts.

Switch to color D.

Rnds 39–42: Sc in each sc.

Stuff the body, using polyester fiberfill or PVC pellets.

Now the body will be divided to form the legs. Place the working yarn loop on a locking stitch marker. You should have a head with a tubular body and arms attached.

Find the center front point. This point lies along the lower edge of the body and lines up with the nose of your creature. Place a pin (large-headed seaming pins are particularly useful for this) or stitch marker between two stitches to mark center front point. Count 18 stitches on either side of the center point. Place a second stitch marker or pin between two stitches at the center back. The center front and back points divide the body into a left half and a right half.

Left Leg and Pant

Pant: Put working loop back on hook. Begin working pant leg as follows.

Rnd 1: Sc in each sc to the center back marker, skip next 18 sts (leaving them for Right Leg), remove markers, sc in each sc to the end of the round (18 sts).

Rnds 2–4: Sc in each sc.

Rnd 5: Inc 1 sc (19 sc).

Rnd 6: Sc in each sc.

Rnds 7–10: Rep rnds 5 and 6 twice (21 sc).

Switch to 3.75mm/F-5 hook.

Rnd 11: Inc 1 sc (22 sc).

Rnd 12: Working through FLO, sc in each sc.

Rnds 13–16: Rep rnds 5 and 6 twice (24 sc at end of rnd 16).

Rnds 17–26: Sc in each sc.

Rnd 27: Sl st in each sc.

Fasten off, leaving an 18"/45.7cm tail. Weave in end.

Leg: Roll pant leg back to expose back loop of rnd 11. Pull up a loop of color A in last stitch of rnd 11 and begin working leg as follows.

Rnd 12: Working into unused loop of rnd 11, sc in first st of rnd 11 and in next 21 st. Your last sc goes in the st you joined yarn in (22 sts).

Rnds 13–28: Sc in each sc.

Rnd 29: Sc in each sc to 2 sc before marker, 3 hdc in next sc, hdc in next sc, (next sc should be marked), remove marker and hdc in next sc, hdc in next sc, 3 hdc in next sc, sc in each sc to end of rnd (26 sts).

Rnd 30: Sc in each st until 2nd hdc of rnd 29, 3 hdc in next st, hdc in next 5 sts, 3 hdc in next st, sc in each st to end of rnd (30 sts).

Rnd 31: Sc in each sc until 2nd hdc of rnd 30, 3 hdc in next st, hdc in next 7 sts, 3 hdc in next st, sc in each st to end of rnd (34 sts).

Rnd 32: Sc in each sc until 2nd hdc of rnd 31, 3 hdc in next st, hdc in next 9 sts, 3 hdc in next st, sc in each st to end of rnd (38 sts).

Fasten off, leaving an 18"/45.5cm tail. Weave in end. Stuff the leg, using polyester fiberfill.

Right Leg and Pant

With the 'gurumi's back facing you, sk 7 st. Join color A in next sc.

Rnd 1: Sc in each sc around (18 sts).

Rnds 2–31: Work as for rnds 2–32 of Left Leg and Pant.

Fasten off, leaving an 18"/45.5cm tail. Weave in end. Stuff the leg, using polyester fiberfill.

Sole of Foot (make 2)

Note: Soles of feet are worked in joined, oval-shaped rnds. Ch 1 at beginning of rnds counts as a stitch.

With 3mm/D-3 hook and color D, ch 7.

Rnd 1: Working in back bumps of foundation ch, sc in second ch from hook, sc in next 4 ch, 3 hdc in last ch; working along opposite side of beginning ch, sc in next 5 ch; join with sl st in first sc (14 sts).

Rnd 2: Ch 1, 2 sc in same st as join, sc in next 4 sts, 3 hdc in next st, hdc in next st, 3 hdc in next st, sc in next 4 sts, 3 sc in last st, join with sl st in first sc (21 sts).

Rnd 3: Ch 1, 2 sc in same st as join, sc in next 6 sts, 3 hdc in next st, hdc in next 3 sts, 3 hdc in next st, sc in next 8 sts, join with sl st in first sc (26 sts).

Rnd 4: Ch 1, 2 sc in same st as join, sc in next 8 st, 3 hdc in next st, hdc in next 5 sts, 3 hdc in next st, sc in next 8 sts, 2 sc in next st, join with sl st in first sc (32 sts).

Rnd 5: Ch 1, sc in same st as join, 2 sc in next st, sc in next 9 st, 3 hdc in next st, hdc in next 7 sts, 3 hdc in next st, sc in next 9 sts, 2 sc in next st, sc in next st, do not join (38 sts).

Fasten off leaving a 36"/91.4cm tail. Make invisible join as illustrated on page 26. Do not weave in end. Instead, use it to whipstitch one sole onto each leg, making sure to line up corners of 3 hdcs. Stuff the foot, making sure as you do this that there is enough stuffing in the leg and that the corners at the front of the feet are filled out.

Tail (make 1)

With the pom-pom maker, make a very firm pom-pom that is half color A and half color D. Trim into a nice, round ball and sew in place.

Tip: Tying very full pom-poms can be quite difficult. Try using a few strands of sewing thread instead of yarn.

Skull Appliqué

Cut one skull out of felt using the template on page 127 as a guide.

For teeth and skull outline, embroider stem stitch lines using two strands black of embroidery floss.

Sew sequins and seed beads for eye sockets using invisible thread.

Glue the skull to the bunny's T-shirt, using straight pins to keep it in place while it dries.

Striped Skull Cap with Holes for Bunny Ears (make 1)

Note: Cap is worked in a continuous spiral. Do not join rnds. You may wish to use a marker to indicate the beginning of the rnd.

Work through back loop only for entire cap.

With 3.75mm/F-5 hook and color F, mr.

Rnd 1: Ch 1, 6 sc in ring, sl st to top of first sc to join, pull starting ring closed (6 sc).

Change to color G.

Rnd 2: Ch 1, 2 sc in each sc around (12 sc).

Change back and forth between colors F and G every rnd for striped pattern.

Rnds 3–5: Sc around increasing 6 sc evenly spaced around. Avoid placing increases in the same place every round (30 sc at end of rnd 5).

Rnd 6: Ch 1, sc in same space, sc in next 4 st, ch 6, sk 4 st, sc in next 6 st, 2 sc in next st, sc in next 4 st, ch 6, sk 5 st, 2 sc in next st, sc in next 4 st, 2 sc in next st, sc in next 4 st (36 sts).

Rnd 7: Sc around increasing 6 sc evenly spaced around (42 sc).

Rnd 8–11: Sc in each sc.

Fasten off, weave in ends. Put cap on bunny's head.

This project was made with 1 skein each of

Color A: Caron's Simply Soft (100% acrylic, 3 oz/100g, 166yd/152m), in #2680, Black

Color B: Bernat's Satin (100% acrylic, 3.5oz/100g, 166yd/152m), in #04007, Silk

Color C: Caron's Simply Soft (100% acrylic, 3 oz/100g, 166yd/152m), in #9737, Lt. Country Peach

Color D: Caron's Simply Soft (100% acrylic, 3 oz/100g, 166yd/152m), in #2603, Papaya

Color E: Caron's Simply Soft (100% acrylic, 3 oz/100g, 166yd/152m), in #2714, Copper Kettle

Color F: Caron's Simply Soft (100% acrylic, 3 oz/100g, 166yd/152m), in #2608, Blue Mint

Color G: Caron's Simply Soft (100% acrylic, 3 oz/100g, 166yd/152m), in #2705, Soft Green

Color H: DMC's Perle Cotton, size 5, in #907, LT Parrot Green

Strawbeary

Congrats! You've reached the end of the book and, perhaps, the most challenging pattern. I hope you find her just as sweet as the berries she is named after.

Skill Level
Advanced

Finished Measurements
Approx 12½"/31.8cm tall

You Will Need
Worsted weight "soft-type" acrylic yarn
  Color A: pink
  Color B: lime green
  Color C: light aqua
  Color D: red
  Color E: navy
  Color F: cream
  Color G: burgundy
Perle cotton, size 5
  Color H: white
Eyelash yarn
  Color I: red
See page 10 for tips on estimating yarn amounts.
Crochet hooks:
  3.5mm/E-4 or size to obtain gauge
  3mm/D-3
  3.75mm/F-5
  4mm/G-6
  1.4mm/9 steel hook
Tapestry needle
Polyester fiberfill
PVC pellets (optional)
Knee-high nylon (if using PVC pellets)
2 eyes of any color, 9mm (for arm joints)
2 dark brown eyes, 12mm
Fine-tooth comb
Locking stitch markers

Embroidery needle
Perle cotton, light red
Perle cotton, black
Invisible thread
Sewing needle
Large-headed seaming pins
2 silver brads (paper fasteners)
1 strawberry-shaped button, approx ½"/1.3cm

Caution: The brads and PVC pellets listed above are
  not child-safe. If you're making this project for a
  child, omit the brads and use polyester fiberfill for
  stuffing.

Gauge
5 rnd gauge circle = 2"/5cm
See page 32 for instructions on making a gauge circle.

Stitches and Techniques Used
Make ring (mr), page 17
Chain (ch)
Single crochet (sc)
Invisible Decrease (invdec), page 23
Bobble, page 22
Slip stitch (sl st)
Changing colors, page 29
Double crochet (dc)
Half double crochet (hdc)
Front loop only (FLO)
French knot, page 30

Instructions

Note: Sometimes, before or after a color change, I work an uncounted rnd of sl sts as indicated in the instructions. Do not work back into the sl sts. Instead, work the next rnd into the loops at the top of the rnd below. This smoothes out the color change. Be careful to keep your stitch count correct. If you find this difficult, you can skip these rows and work chain stitch embroidery to cover the color change after you are finished crocheting the doll. It gives the same effect but leaves more ends to weave in.

Arm (make 2)

Note: Arms are worked in a continuous spiral. Do not join rnds. You may wish to use a marker to indicate the beginning of the rnd.

Starting at fingertips, with 3.5mm/E-4 hook and color A, mr.

Rnd 1: Ch 1, work 6 sc in ring, pull starting ring closed (6 sc).

Rnd 2: 2 sc in each sc around (12 sc).

Rnd 3: *2 sc in next sc, sc in next sc; rep from * around (18 sc).

Rnds 4 and 5: Sc in each sc.

Rnd 6: Sc in next 16 sc, invdec over last 2 sc (17 sts).

Rnd 7: Sc in next 7 sts, invdec over next 2 sts, sc in next 7 sts, make bobble in next st (16 sts).

Rnd 8: Sc in next 14 sts, invdec over next 2 sts (15 sts).

Rnd 9: Invdec over next 2 sts, sc in next 13 sts (14 sts).

Switch to color B. Work and uncounted rnd of sl st.

Rnd 10: Sc in next 6 sts, invdec over next 2 sts, sc in next 6 sts (13 sts).

Switch to color C.

January 16

Shoes are a Girl's Best Friend

Mary Janes are far and away my favorite type of shoe. In fact I have a pair of red ones just like Strawbeary's. I love them and save them for special occasions. I don't want to wear them out.

117

Rnd 11: Sc in next 11 sts, invdec over next 2 sts (12 sts).

Switch back and forth between colors B and C every rnd for stripe pattern.

Rnd 12: Sc in next 4 sts, invdec over next 2 sts, sc in next 6 sts (11 sts).

Rnd 13: Sc in next 9 sts, invdec over next 2 sts (10 sts).

Rnds 14–33: Sc in each sc around, continuing to change colors for stripe pattern.

Fasten off, leaving an 18"/45.7cm tail. Stuff arm. To make the shoulder joint, put a 9mm eye inside each arm with the shaft poking out in the first valley down from the top, lining up with the bobble thumb. Put a bit more stuffing on top of the shoulder. Close hole as illustrated in on page 26. Weave in ends. Use an 18"/45.7cm length of yarn to sew through both layers of the arm to create a dent for the elbow in the 12th valley down from the top.

Pointed Eye Patches (make 2)

Starting at center of Eye Patch, with 1.4mm/9 steel hook and color H, mr. Leave starting ring large so eye can be inserted.

Rnd 1: Ch 3 (counts as 1 dc), 13 dc in ring, join with sl st in top of beginning ch-3, do not pull starting ring closed (14 sts).

Rnd 2: Ch 2, hdc in same space as join, hdc in next st, sc in next st, (hdc, dc, hdc, in next st), sc in the next st, hdc in the next st, 2 hdc in next st, 2 dc in next 7 sts, do not join (24 sts).

Fasten off, leaving a 12"/30.5cm tail. Make invisible join as illustrated on page 26. Weave in end.

Insert eye shaft into ring. Pull gently on tail of starting ring to snug around eye shaft. Set aside for later.

Ear (make 2)

Note: Ears are worked in a continuous spiral. Do not join rnds. You may wish to use a marker to indicate the beginning of the rnd.

With 3.5mm/E-4 hook and color D, mr.

Rnd 1: Ch 1, work 6 sc in ring; do not join (6 sc).

Rnd 2: 2 sc in each sc around (12 sc).

Rnd 3: (Sc in next sc, 2 sc in next sc) 6 times (18 sc).

Rnd 4: (Sc in next 7 sc, invdec over next 2 sts) twice (16 sts).

Rnd 5: (Sc in next 6 sc, invdec over next 2 sts) twice (14 sts).

Rnd 6: (Sc in next 5 sc, invdec over next 2 sts) twice (12 sts).

Rnd 7: (Sc in next 4 sc, invdec over next 2 sts) twice (10 sts).

Fasten off, leaving a long tail for sewing ear to head. Flatten ear and fold in half. There should be four layers of crochet. Using yarn tail to whipstitch these layers together. Leave remaining length of yarn to sew tail to body. Set aside for later.

Wig (make 1)

Note: Wig is worked in a continuous spiral. Do not join rnds. You may wish to use a marker to indicate the beginning of the rnd.

With 4.25mm/G-6 hook and color I, mr.

Rnd 1: Ch 1, work 6 sc in ring (6 sc).

Rnd 2: 2 sc in each sc around (12 sc).

Rnds 3–7: Sc around increasing 6 sc evenly spaced (42 sc at end of rnd 7).

Rnds 8–12: Sc in each sc.

119

Fasten off. Weave in end. Using a fine-tooth comb, comb out the ends of the eyelash yarn to right side of the crochet. Otherwise, too much of the texture will be on the wrong side and it won't look like much of a wig. Set aside for later.

Body (make 1)

Note: Body is worked in a continuous spiral. Do not join rnds. You may wish to use a marker to indicate the beginning of the rnd.

Starting at top of head, with 3.5mm/E-4 hook and color A, mr.

Rnd 1: Ch 1, work 6 sc in ring (6 sc).

Rnd 2: 2 sc in each sc around (12 sc).

Rnds 3–5: Sc around increasing 6 sc evenly spaced around. Avoid placing increases in the same place every round (30 sc at end of rnd 5).

Rnds 6–13: Sc around increasing 3 sc evenly spaced around (54 sc at end of rnd 13).

Rnds 14 and 15: Sc in each sc.

Rnd 16–19: Sc around, invdec 6 times evenly spaced. Avoid placing decreases in the same place every round (30 sts at end of rnd 19).

Rnd 20: (Invdec over next 2 sts) 15 times (15 sts).

Place working yarn loop on a locking stitch marker or safety pin and position the yarn tail at the back of the head. You 'll now assemble the head.

The eyes are set in place first. If you look at the texture of the crochet you'll see that the rounds form ridges and valleys. If you look even closer at the texture you'll see tiny posts in the valleys between rounds. Place the eyes in the third valley above the first decrease round. Another way of saying this is to put them between rounds 13 and 14, thirteen posts apart, making sure eyes are centered in the doll's face. Once you know where you want the eyes to be, use something like the end of a rattail comb to poke a large hole into the crochet. Don't worry about hurting the crochet; it should be quite strong since you used such a small hook. Poke the eye shafts through to the inside of the head and fasten with the washers that came with them. Referring to photo as a guide, use light red Perle cotton to embroider eyebrows. Use black Perle cotton to embroider the muzzle.

Pin wig onto head, stretching it to fit nicely around the face and neck. Sew it to head with invisible thread. Using the yarn tails you left on the ears and a tapestry needle, sew them in place right through the wig and onto the head. Weave the ends in to the head.

For both the ears and the wig, it is helpful to stuff the head first, pin these things in place using large-headed pins, and then sew them on.

Make sure the head is stuffed firmly. After the head is rounded out, tack the eye patches down with invisible thread as well.

Replace working loop on hook and switch to color C.

Work an uncounted rnd of sl sts.

Rnd 21: Sc around, inc 3 sc evenly spaced around (18 sc).

Rnd 22: Sc in each st.

Rnds 23 and 24: Rep rnds 21 and 22 (21 sc at end of rnd 24).

To attach arms, put the eye shafts at the shoulders into body in the valley between rnds 22 and 23, eleven posts apart in the front. Put washers on eye shafts to secure arms.

Rnds 25–34: Rep last 2 rnds 5 times (36 sc at end of rnd 34).

Rnds 35–37: Sc in each sc.

Work an uncounted rnd of sl sts.

Skirt

Switch to 3.75mm/F-5 hook and color E.

Rnd 1: Working through FLO, sc in each sc.

Rnds 2–8: Work through both loops, sc in each sc.

Rnd 9: Sl st in each sc around.

Fasten off. Weave in ends.

Roll skirt back to expose back loop of rnd 37. Pull up a loop of color F in last stitch of rnd 37 and proceed with rnd 38.

121

Rnd 38–41: Sc in each sc around.

Work an uncounted rnd of sl sts.

Switch to color A.

Rnd 42: Sc in each sc.

Stuff the body, using polyester fiberfill or PVC pellets.

Now the body will be divided to form the legs. Place the working yarn loop on a locking stitch marker. You should have a head with a tubular body and arms attached.

Find the center front point. This point lies along the lower edge of the body and lines up with the nose of your creature. Place a pin (large-headed seaming pins are particularly useful for this) or stitch marker between two stitches to mark center front point. Count 18 stitches on either side of the center point. Place a second stitch marker or pin between two stitches at the center back. The center front and back points divide the body into a left half and a right half.

Left Leg

Put working loop back on hook.

Rnd 1: Sc in each sc to the center back marker, skip next 18 sts (leaving them for Right Leg), remove markers, sc in each sc to the end of the round (18 sts).

Rnds 2–20: Sc in each sc.

Rnd 21: Sc in each sc around, inc once (19 sts).

Rnd 22: Sc in each sc.

Rnds 23–28: Rep last 2 rnds 3 times (22 sts).

Mark center front stitch of leg with pin or stitch marker.

Rnd 29: Sc in each sc to 2 sc before marker, 3 hdc in next sc, hdc in next sc, (next sc should be marked), remove marker and hdc in next sc, hdc in next sc, 3 hdc in next sc, sc in each sc to end of rnd (26 sts).

Switch to color F.

Work an uncounted rnd of sl sts.

Rnd 30: Sc in each st until 2nd hdc of rnd 29, 3 hdc in next st, hdc in next 5 sts, 3 hdc in next st, sc in each st to end of rnd (30 sts).

Rnd 31: Sc in each sc until 2nd hdc of rnd 30, 3 hdc in next st, hdc in next 7 sts, 3 hdc in next st, sc in each st to end of rnd (34 sts).

Rnd 32: Sc in each sc until 2nd hdc of rnd 31, 3 hdc in next st, hdc in next 9 sts, 3 hdc in next st, sc in each st to end of rnd (38 sts).

Fasten off, leaving an 18"/45.7cm tail. Weave in end. Stuff the leg, using polyester fiberfill.

Right Leg

With the 'gurumi's back facing you, sk 7 st. Join color A in next sc.

Rnd 1: Sc in each sc around (18 sts).

Rnds 2-32: Work as for rnds 2–32 of Left Leg.

Fasten off, leaving an 18"/45.7cm tail. Weave in end. Stuff the leg, using polyester fiberfill.

Strap for Mary Janes (make 2)

Leaving a 12"/30.5cm starting tail, with 3mm/D-3 hook and color F, ch 13.

Fasten off leaving a 12"/30.5cm tail. Sew across the front of the leg in the uncounted rnd of sl sts after rnd 29, approx 13 stitches apart. Insert brad into the stitch that you attach strap in on the outside of the leg. Pinch open arms of brads firmly.

Sole of Foot (make 2)

Note: Soles of feet are worked in joined, oval-shaped rnds. Ch 1 at beginning of rnds counts as a stitch.

With 3mm/D-3 hook and color D, ch 7.

Rnd 1: Working in back bumps of foundation ch, sc in second ch from hook, sc in next 4 ch, 3 hdc in last ch; working along opposite side of beginning ch, sc in next 5 ch; join with sl st in first sc (14 sts).

Rnd 2: Ch 1, 2 sc in same st as join, sc in next 4 sts, 3 hdc in next st, hdc in next st, 3 hdc in next st, sc in next 4 sts, 3 sc in last st, join with sl st in first sc (21 sts).

Rnd 3: Ch 1, 2 sc in same st as join, sc in next 6 sts, 3 hdc in next st, hdc in next 3 sts, 3 hdc in next st, sc in next 8 sts, join with sl st in first sc (26 sts).

Rnd 4: Ch 1, 2 sc in same st as join, sc in next 8 st, 3 hdc in next st, hdc in next 5 sts, 3 hdc in next st, sc in next 8 sts, 2 sc in next st, join with sl st in first sc (32 sts).

Rnd 5: Ch 1, sc in same st as join, 2 sc in next st, sc in next 9 st, 3 hdc in next st, hdc in next 7 sts, 3 hdc in next st, sc in next 9 sts, 2 sc in next st, sc in next st, do not join (38 sts).

Fasten off, leaving a 36"/91.4cm tail. Make invisible join as illustrated on page 26. Do not weave in end. Instead, use it to whipstitch one sole onto each leg, making sure to line up corners of 3 hdcs. Stuff the foot, making sure as you do this that there is enough stuffing in the leg and that the corners at the front of the feet are filled out.

Finishing

To make knees, sew a dent back and forth across the front of each leg with a short length of color A between rnds 10 and 11, five posts apart. Tie in a tight knot, then weave in ends.

With a short length of color F, whipstitch back and forth between the legs to pinch the uncounted rnd of sl sts after rnd 41 of body together. Weave in ends.

Using a 12"/30.5cm strand of color C and tapestry needle, sew strawberry button onto front of T-shirt. Weave in ends.

This project was made with 1 skein each of

Color A: Caron's Simply Soft (100% acrylic, 3.5oz/100g, 166yd/152m), in #2614, Soft Pink

Color B: Caron's Simply Soft (100% acrylic, 3.5oz/100g, 166yd/152m), in #2607, Limelight

Color C: Caron's Simply Soft (100% acrylic, 3.5oz/100g, 166yd/152m), in #2705, Soft Green

Color D: Red Heart's Soft (100% acrylic, 5oz/140g, approx 256yd/234m), in #5142, Cherry Red

Color E: Caron's Simply Soft (100% acrylic, 3.5oz/100g, 166yd/152m), in #2628, Dk. Country Blue

Color F: Bernat's Satin (100% acrylic, 3.5oz/100g, 166yd/152m), in #04007, Silk

Color G: Caron's Simply Soft (100% acrylic, 3.5oz/100g, 166yd/152m), in #2721, Autumn Red

Color H: DMC's Perle Cotton, size 5, in #0000, White

Color I: Yarn Bee's Party Girl (3.5oz/100g, 180yd/165m), in #116, Teresa

Taking Care of Your Hands

Massage

Use the thumb of your left hand to knead the palm of your right, while at the same time wrapping the left fingers around the right hand to rub its back. Massage for one minute, then reverse positions to work the left hand (figure 1).

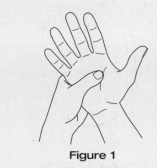

Figure 1

Stretches

Hold your hands out in front of you with elbows comfortably bent. Rotate your wrists gently clockwise, then counterclockwise. Repeat five times (figure 2).

Clench each hand in a tight fist, holding it this way for five seconds. Release, extend the fingers and thumb completely, and hold the stretch for five seconds. Repeat five times (figure 3).

Hook your right thumb with the left hand, and pull it gently down toward the right forearm. You should feel the stretch at the base of the right thumb, at the palm. Hold for five seconds, then stretch the left thumb. Repeat five times, alternating hands (figure 4).

Hold your right hand out in front of you with the fingertips together and pointing up, and the palm facing out. Use the left hand to pull the right fingers gently back toward you, holding the position for five seconds. You should feel this stretch in the wrist. Switch hands, then repeat five times for each side (figure 5).

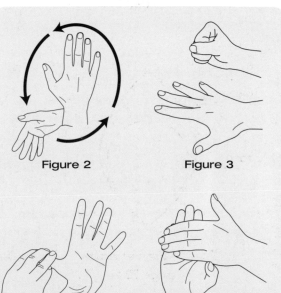

Figure 2

Figure 3

Figure 4

Figure 5

Templates

All 100%

Piglet, page 73
Front Feet

Piglet, page 73
Rear Feet

Werner the Wiener Dog,
page 65

Outer

Inner

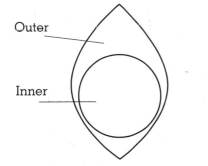

Friends Forever Fawn,
page 79

Benny the Monkey, page 97

Strawbeary, page 115

Punk Bunny, page 106

Index

Abbreviations, 31

Animal projects, 60–85

Assembling dolls, 27

Blanket stitch, 30

Bobble, 22

Chain stitch, 16, 30

Changing color or yarn, 29

Closing hole of remaining stitches, 26

Crab stitch, see reverse single crochet

Crochet hook letter sizes and metric equivalent chart, 9

Crochet stitches, 18–23

Counting chain stitches, 17

Counting rounds and stitches, 25–26

Double crochet, 20

Embellishments, 13–16

Embroidery stitches, 30

Estimating yarn amounts, 10

Eyes, 13

Food projects, 34–59

French knot, 30

Front post double crochet, 22

Gauge, 32–33

Half double crochet, 20

Hands, taking care of your, 29, 126

Hooks, 8–9

Humanoid projects, 86–125

Increases and decreases, 23

Invisible decrease, 23

Invisible join, 26

Joined rounds, 24

Joined, turned rounds, 25

Making rings, 17

Materials, 8–15

Notions, 12–13

Perle cotton, 14

Reverse single crochet, 19

Satin stitch, 30

Seed beads, 15

Single crochet, 19

Single crochet decrease, 23

Slip stitch, 18

Sparkle, 14–15

Special techniques, 28–31

Spirals, 24

Stem stitch, 30

Stitches and techniques, 16–31

Stringing beads onto yarn, 29

Stuffing, 11–12

Templates, 127

Tips for making dolls, 24–26

Treble crochet, 21

Universal gauge circle, 32–33

Working in rounds and spirals, 24

Yarn, 10

Author Bio

Elisabeth A. Doherty received her B.A. in Fine Art from Columbia College and has been at the forefront of developing amigurumi into a fine art form. Her dolls and soft sculptures have been featured in *CRAFT* magazine and numerous art shows across the United States. Please visit her at www.gourmetamigurumi.com.

A Note about Suppliers

Usually, the supplies you need for making the projects in Lark books can be found at your local craft supply store. Occasionally, however, you may need to buy materials or tools from specialty suppliers. In order to provide you with the most up-to-date information, we have created a list of suppliers on our website. Visit us at www.larkbooks.com, click on "Craft Supply Sources," and then click on the relevant topic.